HPBooks

Everything But The
KITCHEN SINK

A Plan-Ahead Cookbook

**by Karine Eliason,
Nevada Harward
& Madeline Westover**

Karine Eliason, Madeline Westover & Nevada Harward

Karine Eliason, Madeline Westover and Nevada Harward, authors of the best-selling *Make-a-Mix Cookery* and *More Make-a-Mix Cookery,* have added another cookbook to their list of accomplishments, *Everything But The Kitchen Sink Cookbook.* They were convinced they had the answer to a problem shared by millions of people—how to save time, money and energy in the kitchen.

The authors have taken the frustrations out of routine everyday meal preparation by showing you how to plan ahead to eliminate last-minute meal hassle and how to save on your food dollar. They cover planning ahead for abundant produce, planning ahead for more than one meal, and how to use leftovers in creative ways. The recipes minimize complicated food techniques while presenting traditional and creative methods of preparing fine food.

Karine, Madeline and Nevada make their home in central Arizona, where they all do volunteer work in youth and women's organizations. Wherever they go they are recognized as the *mix ladies.* They have lectured extensively throughout the United States, appearing on TV, radio programs and demonstrating before large audiences. With their busy schedule and large families—they have 18 children among them—they get everyone involved in planning meals ahead.

COVER PHOTOS: Seafood Creole Gumbo, page 55; Fruited Turkey Salad, page 70; and Strawberry-Rum-Cream Cake, page 104.

CONTENTS

ANOTHER BEST-SELLING VOLUME FROM HPBooks®

Publisher: Rick Bailey; Executive Editor: Randy Summerlin
Editorial Director: Elaine R. Woodard; Editor: Rebecca LaBrum
Art Director: Don Burton; Book Design: Kathleen Koopman
Typography: Cindy Coatsworth, Michelle Carter
Director of Manufacturing: Anthony B. Narducci
Food Stylist: Marilyn Berry
Photography: Borge Andersen & Associates

Special thanks go to Felt-Bruchorns, Salt Lake City, Utah,
for their generous loan of props for use in photography.

Published by HPBooks, Inc.
P.O. Box 5367, Tucson AZ 85703   602/888-2150
ISBN 0-89586-370-7
Library of Congress Catalog Card Number 85-81839
©1986 HPBooks, Inc.   Printed in the U.S.A.
1st Printing

General Introduction

This is a book about cooking to save time and money—about thrifty cooking that makes use of "everything but the kitchen sink." Every chapter shows you ways to use your kitchen time efficiently and take better advantage of your food dollars. We also devote plenty of attention to the problem of leftovers. With this book's help, you'll learn to turn your "throwaways" into delicious, economical meals.

Thrifty, time-saving cookery begins with careful planning. Eventually, everyone who cooks realizes that life can be much simpler if menus are devised ahead of time and preparation is done in advance. Planning ahead can all but eliminate the last-minute hassle and frustration that often accompanies mealtime.

One good way to start your menu-planning is to focus on fresh produce in season. In Chapter 1, we suggest a number of uses for more than 50 different fruits and vegetables; we also include a recipe selection and a chart indicating the best time of year to purchase these items. Plan ahead to use each type of produce as it comes into season. You'll save money as well as treat your family to foods at their peak of freshness.

Efficiency in the kitchen is greatly boosted by working smarter, not harder. Let our "Plan-Overs" chapter show you how to save time and money by cooking large cuts of meat—beef, pork, ham, turkey—then dividing the meat for use in many meals. Ham, for example, makes its first appearance as a simple baked ham with cherry sauce; the leftover meat can go into jambalaya, ham loaf, an elegant puff-pastry pie, and more. This style of cooking is one of the best ways to get your money's worth from the meat you buy.

If you're employed out of the home, you'll especially appreciate "Big-Batch" cookery and "Prepare Now, Serve Later." These are recipes you can easily cook in quantity or assemble far in advance, then refrigerate or freeze until needed. Make-ahead dinners are great energy-savers: when you arrive home tired and hungry, you can just pop your meal into the oven and let it cook while you relax.

No book about money-saving cookery would be complete without a discussion of leftovers. They're a kitchen dilemma that's impossible to avoid, no matter how carefully we plan. Naturally, the problem is less serious in a large family whose members are prone to raid the refrigerator searching for after-school or bedtime snacks. Unfortunately, though, a partial can of tomato paste, half a bell pepper or an overripe banana aren't always very appealing to the appetite! Americans throw out billions of dollars worth of food each year, and that total increases when you consider energy dollars spent to raise, package, transport and store the food in the first place.

Our solution to this ever-present problem is to anticipate waste and avoid it. We suggest keeping a number of quick, easy basic recipes on hand to rescue those little tidbits from the back of the refrigerator before they start turning fuzzy and green. Our "Basic Nine" recipes will accommodate all the typical odds and ends you might have, from meats to hard-cooked eggs to spoonfuls of vegetables and fruits. In fact, one recipe of the Basic Nine, Kitchen-Sink Cookies, is guaranteed to use just about *any* edible leftovers. Tossed salad, pastas, vegetables, casseroles, stews and most other things can be incorporated into these spicy cookies.

Following the Basic Nine, you'll find a Leftover Encyclopedia. Here are more ideas and recipes for using a number of common leftovers, such as mashed potatoes, cooked cereals, egg whites and egg yolks. We also suggest uses for some items that are usually discarded without a second thought. Many people peel potatoes and throw away the nutritious peels. Or they discard the brine from pickles or pour the juices from canned vegetables and fruits down the drain. Some of us probably have the healthiest garbage disposers in town! If you're serious about decreasing your food budget, consult the Leftover Encyclopedia before you throw anything away.

Everything But The Kitchen Sink is written for those cooks interested in saving time, money and energy in the kitchen. There are many plan-ahead dishes for fuss-free entertaining. It is our method for preparing good food efficiently, with little or no waste. It includes recipes for family fare as well as make ahead entertaining ideas. We think you'll agree that *anyone* can make *everything* into *something*.

CHAPTER ONE

Encyclopedia of Abundant Produce

In order to take full advantage of abundant fresh produce, you need to decide ahead of time how you'll use it. When your garden yields bushels of tomatoes or baskets of zucchini, don't beg your friends to take them off your hands; instead, head for the kitchen and stir up a kettle of Grandma Child's Chunky Chili Sauce or a big batch of Fried Zucchini. You'll find both recipes in this chapter, as well as many other ideas for using a variety of fruits and vegetables—whether homegrown or purchased from the market at seasonal bargain prices. We also include a chart to help you in wise monthly meal-planning. It indicates the best time of year to buy a number of produce items.

As each fruit and vegetable comes into season, be on the lookout for grocery-store specials and plan to buy in quantity. Serve some of each season's bounty right away; put up the rest in sauces, soups and preserves to enjoy through the year. By planning wisely, we can avoid the waste that sometimes accompanies the reduced prices and abundance of food items.

Seasonal Guide for Purchasing Fresh Produce

The following chart helps to identify the peak season for most produce. Cost is usually less at these times.

Commodity	JAN	FEB	MAR	APR	MAY	JUN	JUL	AUG	SEP	OCT	NOV	DEC
Apples	✔	✔	✔	✔					✔	✔	✔	✔
Apricots						✔	✔					
Artichokes			✔	✔	✔							
Asparagus		✔	✔	✔								
Avocados	✔									✔	✔	✔
Calif. varieties		✔	✔	✔	✔							
Bananas			✔									
Beans (green, Italian, wax)			✔	✔	✔	✔	✔					
Beets					✔	✔	✔	✔	✔			
Berries												
Blackberries						✔	✔	✔				
Blueberries						✔	✔	✔				
Raspberries						✔	✔	✔				
Strawberries					✔	✔	✔					
Broccoli				✔								
Brussels sprouts										✔	✔	
Cabbage,												
green, red, Savoy,	✔	✔	✔	✔	✔	✔					✔	✔
Chinese (napa cabbage)	✔	✔	✔	✔						✔	✔	✔
Carrots	✔	✔	✔	✔								
Cauliflower										✔	✔	
Celeriac (celery root)	✔	✔	✔						✔	✔	✔	✔
Cherries, sweet & tart					✔	✔						
Citrus												
Grapefruit	✔	✔	✔	✔	✔						✔	✔
Lemons	✔	✔		✔	✔	✔						✔
Limes						✔	✔	✔	✔			
Oranges	✔	✔	✔	✔	✔							✔
Corn			✔	✔	✔	✔	✔					
Cranberries									✔	✔	✔	
Cucumbers						✔	✔	✔				
Grapes, seedless (green or red)						✔	✔	✔	✔			
Greens												
(beet, collard, dandelion,												
mustard, sorrel, turnip)	✔	✔	✔	✔						✔	✔	✔
Jícama	✔	✔	✔	✔	✔	✔				✔	✔	✔
Leeks		✔	✔	✔	✔	✔	✔	✔	✔			
Mangoes					✔	✔	✔	✔				
Melons												
Cantaloupe						✔	✔	✔	✔			
Honeydew						✔	✔	✔	✔	✔		
Watermelon						✔	✔	✔	✔			
Okra					✔	✔	✔	✔	✔	✔		
Parsley										✔	✔	✔
Peaches					✔	✔	✔	✔				
Pears							✔	✔	✔	✔		
Peas	✔	✔	✔	✔	✔	✔	✔					
Peppers (green or red bell)						✔	✔					
Plums					✔	✔	✔	✔				
Potatoes												
Baking potatoes	✔	✔	✔	✔	✔	✔	✔				✔	✔
New potatoes	✔	✔	✔	✔								
Sweet potatoes										✔	✔	✔
Pumpkins										✔		
Rhubarb		✔	✔	✔	✔							
Rutabaga	✔	✔	✔						✔	✔	✔	✔
Spinach	✔	✔	✔	✔	✔							✔
Squash												
Summer (crookneck,												
pattypan, zucchini)					✔	✔	✔	✔	✔			
Winter (acorn, banana,												
butternut, Hubbard)	✔	✔	✔					✔	✔	✔	✔	✔
Swiss chard						✔	✔	✔	✔			
Tomatoes					✔	✔	✔					

Apples

Suggestions for use: Use in pies, cobblers, fruit crisps, Waldorf salads, fruit cups; use for dumplings, fritters, applesauce, baked apples, apple brown betty, apple butter, apple jelly and cinnamon apple rings.

Recipes included:
A-Z Bread, page 33
Apple Hill Cake, page 12
Apple Crisp, page 12
Curried Turkey Bombay, page 70
Fresh Blender Applesauce, page 13
Fruited Turkey Salad, page 70

Apricots

Suggestions for use: Use in pies, cobblers, cookies, jams, glazes and toppings; use for fruit leather.

Recipes included:
A-Z Bread, page 33
Apricot Crisp, page 12

Artichokes

Suggestions for use: Steam or boil artichokes; remove choke with a metal spoon. Dip cooked leaves in mayonnaise or lemon butter; use hollowed-out cooked artichoke as a dip container. Or stuff hollowed-out cooked artichokes with sautéed onion, crabmeat and dairy sour cream, then sprinkle with Parmesan cheese. Place stuffed artichokes in a casserole dish; bake 10 to 15 minutes in a 350F (175C) oven.

Asparagus

Suggestions for use: Cook and serve with hollandaise sauce, garnished with hard-cooked eggs; cook, roll up in thin ham slices and top with hollandaise or cheese sauce; cook and toss with toasted almonds or croutons; cook, chill and use in chef's salads; use in soups.

Recipes included:
Asparagus with Orange Hollandaise Sauce, page 15
Neptune's Heavenly Garden Salad, page 84

Avocados

Suggestions for use: Use as "bowls" to serve crab, tuna or chicken salad; slice and use as garnish for salads and Mexican dishes; use in guacamole.

Recipes included:
A-Z Bread, page 33
Avocado-Chicken Bake, page 86
Avocado Pie, page 13
Avocado Supreme Dressing, page 116
Guacamole, page 13
Navajo Tacos with Chili Verde Sauce, page 66
Our Favorite Gazpacho, page 80

Bananas

Suggestions for use: Use in cakes, pies, breads, muffins, milkshakes, fruit salads, ice cream, puddings; slice and serve in orange juice as a fruit cup; cut in 1-inch slices, freeze and use as dippers for chocolate fondue.

Recipes included:
A-Z Bread, page 33
Do-Ahead Frozen Fruit Salads, page 40
Frozen Banana-Split Dessert, page 17
Frozen Fruit-Punch Base, page 39
Fruit Dips & Toppers, page 37
Fruited Turkey Salad, page 70
Granny's Banana Cake, page 16
Homemade Fruit Ice Cream, page 36
Margaret's Banana Bread, page 15
Patty's Sour-Cream Muffins, page 16
Strawberry Cream Squares, page 82

Beans (green, Italian, wax)

Suggestions for use: Add to soups, stews and chowders; flavor cooked beans with sautéed bacon bits and fresh tomatoes.

Recipes included:
Green Beans with Almonds, page 18
Puffy Fried Vegetables, page 24

Beets

Suggestions for use: Cook, then slice or julienne and use in salads; cook and flavor with herb butter; use in Harvard beets or pickled beets.

Recipes included:
Beets in Cream Sauce, page 18
Beets in Orange Glaze, page 18

Berries (blackberries, blueberries, raspberries, strawberries)

Suggestions for use: Use in cobblers, muffins, pancakes, pies, syrups, sauces, jams and jellies, ice cream, milkshakes, gelatin salads and desserts; use as a topping for ice cream; serve with Sweet English Custard Sauce, page 136; dip whole strawberries in dairy sour cream, then in brown sugar for a delicious dessert.

Recipes included:
A-Z Bread, page 33
Barbara's English Trifle, page 20
Homemade Fruit Ice Cream, page 36
Mother-in-Law Dessert, page 20
New England Blueberry Pancakes, page 17
Strawberry-Rum-Cream Cake, page 104

Broccoli

Suggestions for use: Use in soups, casseroles, salads; use on relish trays.

Recipes included:
Dill Dip, page 37
Double-Good Baked Broccoli, page 49
Beef-Broccoli Stir-Fry, page 89
Foil Side Dishes, page 95
Herbed-Chicken Foil Dinner, page 87
Our Favorite Cream of Broccoli Soup, page 19
Stir-Fry Vegetable Medley, page 22

Brussels sprouts

Suggestions for use: Cook and serve with cheese sauce; cook and toss with sautéed bread crumbs, chopped hard-cooked eggs and chopped parsley; cook and toss with water chestnuts or jícama for added crunch; chill cooked sprouts and marinate in brine from dill pickles for 12 hours, then serve with wooden picks as an appetizer.

Cabbage (green, red, Savoy)

Suggestions for use: Use in coleslaw, salads and soups; use outer leaves as wrappers for cabbage rolls.

Recipes included:
Cabbage in Cream, page 19
Vegetable Scramble, page 19

Cabbage, Chinese (napa cabbage) or bok choy

Suggestions for use: Slice and use in salads and stir-fry dishes; add to soups or Oriental hot pots.

Recipes included:
Miniature Egg Rolls, page 42

Carrots

Suggestions for use: Use in soups, stews, steamed puddings, cakes, breads, cookies; glaze cooked carrots with butter and brown sugar; shred carrots and toss with pineapple chunks, raisins and mayonnaise for a nutritious salad.

Recipes included:
A-Z Bread, page 33
Carrot Cake, page 23
Carrot-Orange Salad Supreme, page 81
Dill Dip, page 37
Foil Side Dishes, page 95
Ilene's Carrot Ring, page 22
Minted Carrots, page 22
Stir-Fry Vegetable Medley, page 22
"The Works" Oven Stew, page 91

Cauliflower

Suggestions for use: Use raw or parboiled on relish trays; cook and top with grated cheese or cheese sauce.

Recipes included:
Dill Dip, page 37
Puffy Fried Vegetables, page 24

Celeriac (celery root)

Suggestions for use: Cook and peel, then marinate in French dressing, add diced tomatoes and serve on lettuce leaves; cook and peel, then mix with cream sauce, top with cheese and bread crumbs and bake 45 minutes in a 350F (175C) oven; cook and peel, then chill and use in place of celery in Waldorf salads.

Cherries (sweet or tart)

Suggestions for use:
SWEET: Freeze whole, slightly thaw and eat for snacks; use in fruit cups, jams and jellies; use for fruit leather.

TART: Use in pies, cobblers, fillings, glazes, jams and jellies; use for canning.

Recipes included:
A-Z Bread, page 33

Cranberries
Suggestions for use: Use in sauces, breads, muffins and gelatin salads.
Recipes included:
A-Z Bread, page 33
Cranberry-Fruit Salad, page 24

Cucumbers
Suggestions for use: Use in salads; use to make pickles; slice with onion and tomatoes in vinegar-and-water brine, or slice and marinate in dairy sour cream.
Recipes included:
Our Favorite Gazpacho, page 80
Refrigerator Spice Pickles, page 24

Eggplant
Suggestions for use: Dip slices in bread crumbs and fry or bake until tender; cube, steam and top with stewed tomatoes; use in ratatouille and eggplant Parmesan.

Grapefruit
Suggestions for use: Squeeze for juice; for a colorful salad, alternate grapefruit segments with avocado wedges and top with French dressing; broil grapefruit halves with brown-sugar topping.
Recipes included:
Arizona Breakfast Grapefruit, page 25
Grapefruit Slush, page 25

Grapes (green, seedless)
Suggestions for use: Use in salads, fruit cups; frost with beaten egg whites and use as garnish; freeze and eat for snacks, slightly thawed.
Recipes included:
Cranberry-Fruit Salad, page 24
Frozen Fruit Combo, page 52
Fruited Turkey Salad, page 70
Gayle's Chicken Salad, page 73

Greens (beet, collard, dandelion, mustard, sorrel, turnip, kale)
Suggestions for use: Combine with lettuce in tossed green salads; cook and sprinkle with vinegar.

Jícama
Suggestions for use: Eat raw with dips; sliver and use in green salads or fruit cups; use as a substitute for water chestnuts in stir-fry and Oriental dishes.
Recipes included:
Dill Dip, page 37

Kiwifruit
Suggestions for use: Peel, slice and sprinkle with lemon or lime juice. Then use to accompany and garnish fish, poultry, pork and salads such as crab, shrimp, fruit, cottage cheese or coleslaw; add to tossed green salads; use to top tarts or cheesecakes. *Do not* use in gelatin (prevents setting); *do not* add to ice cream or milk products (causes curdling).
Recipes included:
Fruit Dips & Toppers, page 37

Leeks
Suggestions for use: Use as a substitute for green onions or shallots; use in soups, omelets and casseroles.
Recipes included:
Our Favorite Cream of Broccoli Soup, page 19

Lemons & limes
Suggestions for use: Use in lemonade, pies, sauces, fillings, puddings, sherbets, cheesecake; use on seafood.
Recipes included:
Avocado Pie, page 13
Florida Key Lime Soufflé, page 139
Fresh Lemonade Syrup, page 26
Frozen Fruit Combo, page 52
Frozen Fruit-Punch Base, page 39
Lemon Cloud Pie, page 135
Lemon Pot Roast, page 26
Luscious Lemon Ice Cream, page 26

Mangoes
Suggestions for use: Use on fresh fruit plates, in fruit salads and fruit cups; use to make chutney and as a substitute for peaches in some recipes.
Recipes included:
Fruit Dips & Toppers, page 37

Melons (cantaloupe, honeydew, watermelon)

Suggestions for use: Use on fresh fruit plates, in fruit salads and fruit cups; use to make fruit ices; hollow out watermelon and use as a bowl to hold fruit salad; fill seeded cantaloupe halves with ice cream or sherbet, or fill with chicken salad for a special luncheon.

Recipes included:
Fruit Dips & Toppers, page 37

Nectarines

Suggestions for use: Use on fresh fruit plates, in fruit salads and fruit cups; use as a substitute for peaches.

Recipes included:
A-Z Bread, page 33
Fruit Dips & Toppers, page 37

Okra

Suggestions for use: Slice, dip in seasoned flour and fry in hot oil 3 to 5 minutes or until tender; use in soups and gumbos; use to make pickles.

Recipes included:
Seafood Creole Gumbo, page 35

Oranges

Suggestions for use: Squeeze for juice; use in sauces, fruit cups, salads, ambrosia, cakes, frostings, fillings, breads; peel, slice and dust with powdered sugar for a side dish; slice and use as a garnish.

Recipes included:
A-Z Bread, page 33
Asparagus with Orange Hollandaise Sauce, page 15
Carrot-Orange Salad Supreme, page 81
Choco-Orange Cake, page 28
Eggnog-Punch Base, page 75
Frozen Fruit Combo, page 52
Frozen Fruit-Punch Base, page 39
Orange Cookies, page 27
Orange Crescent Rolls, page 99
Orange Syrup, page 28

Papayas

Suggestions for use: Use on fresh fruit plates, in fruit salads and fruit cups; halve and seed, then serve with a squeeze of lemon or lime juice; halve and seed, then fill with fruit sherbet, or fill with shrimp and serve with a lime wedge; sauté in butter to accompany meat or fish dishes; cube and wrap with thin slices of ham as an appetizer; use in tossed green salads.

Recipes included:
Fruit Dips & Toppers, page 37

Parsnips

Suggestions for use: Cook and season with butter, salt, and parsley; cook and glaze with brown sugar and butter or with honey, lemon juice and butter; add to soups and stews.

Peaches

Suggestions for use: Use in pies, cobblers, fruit salads, fruit cups, jams and jellies, ice cream; use as a topping for shortcakes.

Recipes included:
A-Z Bread, page 33
Barbara's English Trifle, page 20
Frozen Fruit Combo, page 39
Fruit Dips & Toppers, page 37
Homemade Fruit Ice Cream, page 36

Pears

Suggestions for use: Use on fresh fruit plates, in salads and fruit cups; use in fresh fruit pie with streusel topping; serve for dessert with sliced mild cheeses.

Recipes included:
A-Z Bread, page 33
Frozen Fruit Combo, page 52
Fruit Dips & Toppers, page 37

Peas

Suggestions for use: Use in soups, stews, salads; combine cooked peas with cream sauce and boiled new potatoes.

Recipes included:
Country Cheese Soup, page 80
"The Works" Oven Stew, page 91

Peppers (green or red bell)

Suggestions for use: Use in salads, omelets, fried rice, salsas, creole sauce; use for stuffed peppers.

Recipes included:
Dill Dip, page 37

Do-Ahead Tomato-Vegetable Soup, page 39
Eldora's Salsa, page 41
Grandma Child's Chunky Chili Sauce, page 35
Our Favorite Gazpacho, page 80

Plums

Suggestions for use: Use in jams and jellies, fruit tarts and kuchens; use for fruit leather.
Recipes included:

Potatoes (baking or new)

Suggestions for use: Use in soups, stews, potato salad; peel, dice and fry in butter for hash browns; use cooked in scalloped potatoes.
Recipes included:
Idaho Stuffed Spudskins, page 30
Mashed-Potato Delight, page 96
Norwegian Lefse, page 141
Potato Nests, page 29
Potato Salad for a Crowd, page 81
"The Works" Oven Stew, page 91
Twice-Baked Potatoes, page 96

Potatoes (sweet or yams)

Suggestions for use: Bake and season with salt, pepper and butter; cook, mash and season with brown sugar, cinnamon and butter; use in stir-fry dishes; cook, top with miniature marshmallows and brown sugar and bake until glazed; use in pies; use uncooked on relish trays. If using raw, slice right before using, since slices will darken; or if prepared ahead, sprinkle cut surfaces lightly with lemon or orange juice.
Recipes included:
Dill Dip, page 37

Pumpkin

Suggestions for use: Use in pies, breads, cookies and cakes.
Recipes included:
A-Z Bread, page 33
Perfect Pumpkin Pie, page 31

Rhubarb

Suggestions for use: Use in cakes, pies, cobblers and jams.
Recipes included:
A-Z Bread, page 33
Rose's Rhubarb Cake, page 30

Rutabagas

Suggestions for use: Cook, puree in a blender or food processor and add to mashed potatoes; cook with carrots until tender, then puree in a blender or food processor with a little butter and whipping cream; then season with ground mace, salt and pepper and top with sautéed onion rings.

Spinach or Swiss chard

Suggestions for use: Use uncooked in salads, topped with crisp-cooked crumbled bacon, hard-cooked eggs and French dressing; use uncooked in stir-fry dishes; use cooked in lasagna, soufflés, crepes, quiches and frittatas.
Recipes included:
Puffy Fried Vegetables, page 24
Raisin-Almond Spinach Salad, page 31

Squash
(Summer: crookneck, pattypan, zucchini—Winter: acorn, banana, butternut, Hubbard)

Suggestions for use:
SUMMER: Use uncooked on relish trays; steam, season and use as a side dish for meat, fish and poultry; steam and mix with white sauce; slice, dip in bread crumbs and fry in hot oil or butter 3 to 5 minutes or until tender; shred and use in quick breads.
WINTER: Bake and top with salt, pepper and butter, or with brown sugar and cinnamon; bake, puree and use in sweet pies.
Recipes included:
A-Z Bread, page 33
Dill Dip, page 37
Foil Side Dishes, page 95
Fried Zucchini, page 32
Low-Cal Chicken-Breast Foil Dinner, page 87
Zucchini Bake, page 32

Tomatoes

Suggestions for use: Use in salads, sandwiches, sauces and stewed tomatoes.
Recipes included:
Do-Ahead Tomato-Vegetable Soup, page 39
Eldora's Salsa, page 41
Grandma Child's Chunky Chili Sauce, page 35
Our Favorite Gazpacho, page 80
Tomatoes Vinaigrette, page 81

Apple Hill Cake

This moist, nutty cake comes from the great State of Washington.

1/2 cup vegetable oil
2 cups sugar
2 eggs
2 teaspoons vanilla extract
1 teaspoon ground cinnamon
2 cups all-purpose flour

1/2 teaspoon salt
1 teaspoon baking soda
1 cup coarsely chopped nuts
4 cups peeled, cored, chopped cooking apples
  (4 large apples)
Creamy Topping, see below

Creamy Topping:
1/2 cup butter or margarine
1/2 cup sugar

1/2 cup evaporated milk

Preheat oven to 350F (175C). Grease and flour a 13'' x 9'' baking pan. In a large bowl, combine oil, sugar, eggs, vanilla and cinnamon. In a medium bowl, sift together flour, salt and baking soda; stir into sugar mixture. Stir in nuts and apples. Pour batter into prepared pan. Bake 50 to 55 minutes or until a wooden pick inserted in center comes out clean. Prepare Creamy Topping; just before cake is finished baking pour over cake. Makes 12 to 15 servings.

Creamy Topping:
In a small saucepan, combine butter or margarine, sugar and evaporated milk. Bring to a boil over medium heat. Cook 5 to 6 minutes, stirring constantly; immediately pour over hot cake.

Apple Crisp

The combination of tender apples and spicy, crispy crust tastes especially wonderful topped with vanilla ice cream or sweetened whipped cream.

6 to 7 cups peeled, cored,
  sliced Golden Delicious apples
  (6 or 7 large apples)
1/4 cup lemon or orange juice
1-3/4 cups sugar
1-3/4 cups all-purpose flour

1-1/2 teaspoons ground cinnamon
1/2 teaspoon ground nutmeg
1/8 teaspoon salt
10 tablespoons butter or margarine
Ice cream or sweetened whipped cream,
  if desired

Preheat oven to 375F (190C). Butter a 13'' x 9'' baking dish. Spread apples evenly in buttered dish. Drizzle lemon or orange juice over apples. In a medium bowl, combine sugar, flour, cinnamon, nutmeg and salt. Cut in butter or margarine with a pastry blender or 2 knives until fine crumbs form. Spread mixture evenly over apples. Bake 45 minutes or until top is golden brown. Serve hot or cold. Top with ice cream or whipped cream, if desired. Makes 8 to 10 servings.

Variations
Apricot Crisp: Substitute 6 to 7 cups sliced apricots for apples.
Peach Crisp: Substitute 6 to 7 cups peeled, sliced peaches for apples.

Fresh Blender Applesauce

When apples are plentiful and inexpensive, try making this easy, fresh-tasting applesauce. It's a good accompaniment for pork dishes.

**4 large cooking apples, peeled,
    cored, cubed (about 4 cups)**
1/4 cup water

2 tablespoons lemon juice
1/3 cup sugar
1/8 teaspoon ground cinnamon, if desired

In a blender or a food processor fitted with a metal blade, combine apples, water, lemon juice, sugar and cinnamon, if desired. Process until mixture is smooth. Transfer mixture to a saucepan; bring to a boil. Serve warm or cool, cover and refrigerate until chilled. Makes 2 cups.

Guacamole   *Photo on page 46.*

After preparing Guacamole with fresh avocados, put avocado pit back into mixture until serving time to help prevent darkening. Serve with Navajo Tacos with Chili Verde Sauce, page 66, or any of your favorite Mexican dishes.

2 ripe avocados, pitted, peeled, mashed
1 teaspoon lemon juice

Salt and black pepper to taste
Few drops of hot-pepper sauce

In a small bowl, combine avocados, lemon juice, salt, black pepper and hot-pepper sauce. Stir until smooth. Cover; refrigerate until ready to serve. Makes about 3/4 cup.

Avocado Pie

Even those who think they don't like avocados like this pie!

1 (14-oz.) can sweetened condensed milk
1 large ripe avocado, pitted, peeled, mashed
1/3 cup lemon juice
1/2 pint whipping cream (1 cup), whipped

**1 (9-inch) Graham-Cracker Pie Crust,
    page 52, or cookie-crumb crust**
3 tablespoons powdered sugar

In a medium bowl, combine sweetened condensed milk, avocado and lemon juice. Fold in half the whipped cream; spoon avocado mixture into crust. Stir powdered sugar into remaining whipped cream; spread on top of pie. Refrigerate at least 3 hours or up to 24 hours. Makes 6 to 8 servings.

Asparagus With Orange Hollandaise Sauce

The sauce adds an extra-special touch to this delicious vegetable.

2 lbs. asparagus, woody ends trimmed
Orange Hollandaise Sauce, see below

Grated orange peel, if desired

Orange Hollandaise Sauce:
4 egg yolks (1/3 cup)
1/4 cup orange juice
1 teaspoon grated orange peel

Salt and pepper to taste
1/2 cup butter, cut in 8 equal pieces
1/2 cup dairy sour cream

Place asparagus on a steaming rack in a saucepan over a small amount of water. Bring to a boil; reduce heat. Cover; steam asparagus 15 to 20 minutes or until tender-crisp. About 5 minutes before asparagus is done, prepare Orange Hollandaise Sauce. Drain asparagus; immediately serve sauce over hot asparagus. Garnish with orange peel, if desired. Makes 4 to 6 servings.

Orange Hollandaise Sauce:
In a small saucepan, combine egg yolks, orange juice, orange peel, salt and pepper, stirring with a whisk to blend. Place over low heat. Add butter, 1 tablespoon at a time, stirring until butter is melted and sauce is thickened. Remove from heat; stir in sour cream. Serve immediately. Makes 1-1/4 to 1-1/2 cups.

Margaret's Banana Bread

This is the Westovers' family favorite, handed down from mother to daughter.

1/2 cup vegetable shortening
1 cup sugar
2 eggs
3 large bananas, mashed (1-1/2 cups)
1 teaspoon vanilla extract

2-1/2 cups all-purpose flour
1 teaspoon baking soda
1/2 teaspoon salt
1/2 cup chopped walnuts

Preheat oven to 350F (175C). Lightly grease and flour 2 (8'' x 4'') loaf pans. In a large bowl, cream shortening and sugar until light and fluffy. Beat in eggs one at a time. Stir in bananas and vanilla. In a medium bowl, combine flour, baking soda, salt and walnuts; beat into creamed mixture. Pour batter into prepared pans. Bake 1 hour or until a wooden pick inserted in center comes out clean. Cool in pans on a rack 5 minutes. Remove from pans; cool completely on rack. Makes 2 loaves.

Asparagus with Orange Hollandaise Sauce

Granny's Banana Cake   Photo on page 21.

Banana frosting adds the finishing touch to this moist, flavorful cake.

2/3 cup vegetable shortening
1/2 cup granulated sugar
1/2 cup packed brown sugar
2 eggs
1 teaspoon vanilla extract
2 cups all-purpose flour
1/2 teaspoon salt

1 teaspoon baking soda
1/2 cup milk
2 large bananas, mashed (1 cup)
1 cup chopped walnuts
Banana Frosting, see below
1/2 cup chopped walnuts

Banana Frosting:
1/2 large banana, mashed (1/4 cup)
2 tablespoons butter or margarine,
   room temperature
1 tablespoon vegetable shortening

1 teaspoon lemon juice
1 (16-oz.) pkg. powdered sugar
   (4 cups unsifted)
Milk, if necessary

Preheat oven to 350F (175C). Grease and flour a 13'' x 9'' baking pan. In a large bowl, cream shortening and sugars. Add eggs, 1 at a time, beating well after each addition. Stir in vanilla. In a medium bowl, stir together flour, salt and baking soda. Add flour mixture to creamed mixture alternately with milk, adding about 1/3 of the flour mixture at a time. Blend in bananas and 1 cup walnuts. Pour batter into prepared pan. Bake 30 to 40 minutes or until a wooden pick inserted in center comes out clean. Cool in pan on a rack. Prepare Banana Frosting; spread over cooled cake. Sprinkle with 1/2 cup chopped walnuts. Makes 12 to 15 servings.

Banana Frosting:
In a medium bowl, combine banana, butter or margarine, shortening, lemon juice and powdered sugar. If necessary, add milk, 1 teaspoon at a time, to give frosting desired spreading consistency.

Patty's Sour-Cream Muffins

Moist, tender banana muffins with a wonderful flavor.

1/2 cup butter or margarine,
   room temperature
1-1/4 cups sugar
2 eggs
1/4 cup dairy sour cream

1 teaspoon baking soda
2 large bananas, mashed (1 cup)
1-1/2 cups all-purpose flour
1 teaspoon vanilla extract
1/2 teaspoon salt

Preheat oven to 350F (175C). Line 18 muffin cups with paper baking cups. In a medium bowl, cream butter or margarine and sugar. Add eggs; beat until light and fluffy. Stir in sour cream, baking soda, bananas, flour, vanilla and salt. Fill muffin cups 2/3 full. Bake 20 to 25 minutes or until tops spring back when lightly touched. Turn out of muffin cups; cool on racks. Makes 18 muffins.

Tip
Muffin batter may be frozen. To freeze, line 18 muffin cups with paper baking cups. Fill 2/3 full with batter; freeze until solid. Remove frozen muffin cups; place in an airtight freezer bag. Freeze up to 3 months. To bake, return frozen cups to muffin pans. Bake as directed above, increasing baking time by 5 minutes.

Frozen Banana-Split Dessert

A new way to "slice" the traditional banana split.

Chocolate Sauce, see below
22 graham-cracker squares, crushed
  (about 1-3/4 cups crumbs)
1/4 cup sugar
1/4 cup butter or margarine, melted

Chocolate Sauce:
1/2 cup butter or margarine
2 cups powdered sugar

4 or 5 large bananas
1/2 gal. strawberry ice cream,
  slightly softened
1 pint whipping cream (2 cups),
  whipped, sweetened

1 (12-oz.) can evaporated milk
1 (6-oz.) pkg. milk-chocolate pieces (1 cup)

Prepare Chocolate Sauce; set aside. Preheat oven to 350F (175C). In a medium bowl, combine crushed crackers, sugar and melted butter or margarine. Press mixture firmly into a 13'' x 9'' baking dish. Bake 7 to 8 minutes. Cool on a rack. Slice bananas evenly over cooled crust. Spoon ice cream evenly over bananas. Top with cooled Chocolate Sauce and whipped cream. Cover; freeze 3 to 4 hours or until firm, or freeze up to 2 months. Makes 12 to 15 servings.

Chocolate Sauce:
In a medium, heavy saucepan, melt butter or margarine over medium heat. Stir in powdered sugar and evaporated milk; blend well. Add chocolate pieces; cook, stirring, until mixture comes to a boil and chocolate pieces are melted. Reduce heat to medium-low; continue to boil, stirring, until thickened. Remove from heat; cool.

New England Blueberry Pancakes

These nutritious whole-wheat pancakes will be a big hit during blueberry season.

2 cups all-purpose flour
2 cups whole-wheat flour
3 tablespoons baking powder
1/4 cup granulated sugar
1-1/2 teaspoons salt
1 qt. milk (4 cups)
2 eggs

1/2 cup vegetable oil
3 tablespoons lemon juice
1/2 teaspoon vanilla extract
1 cup fresh or frozen blueberries
Powdered sugar and additional blueberries; or
honey, pancake syrup or jam

Preheat a large electric griddle to 375F (190C) or heat a large skillet over medium heat. In a large bowl, combine flours, baking powder, granulated sugar and salt. Using a whisk, beat in milk, eggs, oil, lemon juice and vanilla until batter is almost smooth. Carefully fold in 1 cup blueberries. If preparing batter ahead, cover; refrigerate up to 24 hours. To cook, lightly grease hot griddle or skillet. Pour batter on griddle or skillet, using about 1/4 cup for each pancake; spread out to a 4-inch circle. Cook until bottoms of pancakes are golden brown and bubbles begin to break through the surface. Turn pancakes; cook until golden brown on other side. Sprinkle with powdered sugar and additional blueberries, or serve with your favorite honey, syrup or jam. Makes about 30 (4-inch) pancakes.

Tip
When using frozen blueberries in pancakes or muffins, be sure they're still frozen when you fold them into the batter. If thawed, they'll turn the batter blue.

Green Beans with Almonds

A requested favorite when we go to Grandma's house.

2 lbs. green beans, ends and
   strings removed
1 teaspoon salt
1/4 teaspoon white pepper

Dash of garlic powder
3 tablespoons butter or margarine, melted
1/4 cup slivered almonds

Place beans in a medium saucepan; add water to cover. Bring to a boil; boil 1 minute. Reduce heat. Stir in salt, pepper and garlic powder. Cover; cook 15 to 20 more minutes or until tender. Drain. Spoon beans onto a platter. Drizzle with melted butter or margarine; top with almonds. Makes 6 servings.

Beets in Cream Sauce

This side dish is a colorful complement to just about any entree.

1 bunch beets (about 1-1/4 lbs.)
1/2 cup dairy sour cream
2 green onions, thinly sliced

1-1/2 teaspoons white-wine vinegar
1/2 teaspoon sugar
Dash of salt

Cut off beet tops, leaving about 1/4 inch attached to beets. Do not remove beet roots. Rinse beets; place in a medium saucepan. Add water to cover. Bring to a boil; reduce heat. Cover; simmer 30 to 40 minutes or until beets are tender. Pour cooked beets into a colander; cool slightly under cold running water. Remove beet tops; slip off skins by gently rubbing with your hands. Cut peeled beets in half or in quarters; keep warm. In a small saucepan, combine sour cream, green onions, vinegar, sugar and salt. Stir over low heat until mixture is warmed through and sugar is dissolved; do not boil. Spoon over warm beets. Stir, if desired. Makes 4 to 6 servings.

Beets in Orange Glaze

Especially good when made with small, homegrown beets.

1 bunch beets (1-1/2 lbs.)
1/2 teaspoon salt
1-1/2 cups water

1/4 cup butter or margarine
1 orange, sliced
1 cup maple syrup

Cut off beet tops and roots; rinse, scrape and slice beets. In a medium skillet, combine beets, salt and water. Bring to a boil over medium heat; then reduce heat, cover and simmer 10 minutes. Uncover; cook 3 more minutes or until liquid has evaporated. Add butter or margarine, orange slices and maple syrup. Continue to cook 15 more minutes, turning beets to coat with glaze. Serve immediately. Makes 6 servings.

Our Favorite Cream of Broccoli Soup

When broccoli is at its peak, take advantage of the cost savings and serve your family this nutritious soup.

1/4 cup butter or margarine
2/3 cup diced leek (both white
    parts and some green tops)
1/2 cup diced onion
1-1/2 cups diced celery
3 to 3-1/2 cups chopped broccoli flowerets

6 tablespoons all-purpose flour
3 cups chicken broth
1/2 pint half and half (1 cup)
1/8 teaspoon ground thyme
Salt and pepper to taste

In a large saucepan, melt butter or margarine over medium heat. Add leek, onion and celery; sauté 5 minutes or until vegetables are tender-crisp. Add broccoli. Reduce heat to low. Cover; continue to cook 10 to 12 more minutes or until broccoli is almost tender. Blend in flour until evenly distributed. Cook 1 minute or until bubbly. Gradually stir in broth. Bring to a boil; boil, stirring constantly, until slightly thickened. Continue to cook until broccoli is tender. Slowly stir in half and half; heat until soup is hot. Do not boil. Add thyme, salt and pepper; serve hot. Makes 4 to 6 servings.

Cabbage in Cream

A new way to dress up cabbage — mix it with sour cream and just a hint of nutmeg.

1/2 medium head cabbage, shredded
1 egg
1 tablespoon sugar

1/2 cup dairy sour cream
Dash of ground nutmeg

Place cabbage in a large saucepan. Add 2 cups water. Bring to a boil; reduce heat to medium. Cover; simmer 10 to 12 minutes or until cabbage is tender-crisp. Drain in a colander. In a small bowl, combine egg, sugar, sour cream and nutmeg; mix well. Return cabbage to pan; top with sour-cream mixture. Cook, stirring, until heated through. Do not boil. Serve warm. Makes 4 or 5 servings.

Vegetable Scramble

The only way to get some children to eat cabbage!

1/2 medium head cabbage, shredded
2 celery stalks, diced
1/2 green bell pepper, diced
1/2 onion, diced
1/4 cup water

3 medium tomatoes, sliced
2 tablespoons butter or margarine
1 teaspoon salt
1/4 to 1/2 teaspoon black pepper

In a large bowl, toss together cabbage, celery, bell pepper and onion. Place vegetables in a large saucepan; add water. Place tomato slices on vegetables; dot with butter or margarine. Sprinkle with salt and black pepper. Cover; cook over medium-low heat 25 to 30 minutes or until cabbage is tender. Stir gently; serve warm. Makes 6 servings.

Barbara's English Trifle

This recipe came directly from a British sister-in-law.

1 (16-oz.) pkg. frozen unsweetened raspberries, slightly thawed, undrained, or 2 cups fresh raspberries

2 cups sliced fresh peaches mixed with about 1-1/2 tablespoons lemon juice, or 1 (16-oz.) pkg. frozen unsweetened sliced peaches, thawed, undrained

Sugar

1 (1-lb.) pound cake or 1/2 Southern Pound Cake, page 101

3 cups prepared vanilla pudding

Sweetened whipped cream

Sliced almonds, toasted

Reserve about 3/4 cup frozen or fresh whole raspberries for garnish. If using fresh fruit, place peaches and remaining raspberries in separate medium bowls. Sprinkle sugar lightly over fruit. Let stand about 20 minutes or until juices form. Do not sprinkle frozen fruit with sugar. Cut pound cake in 1-inch cubes. In a 3-quart glass bowl, place 1/2 of pound-cake cubes. Next, layer 1/2 of pudding, 1/2 of remaining raspberries and all the peaches over cake cubes. Add remaining cake cubes; sprinkle with all juice from peaches and raspberries. Add remaining pudding. Top with whipped cream and toasted almonds. Cover; refrigerate at least 8 hours or up to 24 hours. Garnish with reserved raspberries. Makes about 12 servings.

Variations

Other fruit combinations, such as sliced strawberries and sliced bananas dipped in lemon juice, may be substituted for peaches and raspberries. Drained canned sliced peaches may also be used in place of fresh or frozen peaches.

Mother-in-Law Dessert

This eye-catching dessert is a great family favorite.

1 (9-oz.) pkg. white-cake mix

1 egg

1/2 cup water

1 cup powdered sugar

1 (8-oz.) pkg. cream cheese, room temperature

1/2 pint whipping cream (1 cup), whipped

2 (4-3/4-oz.) pkgs. strawberry-flavored Danish dessert plus 3 cups water, or 2 (15-oz.) jars strawberry glaze

2 pints strawberries, sliced

Preheat oven to 350F (175C). Grease and flour a 13'' x 9'' baking pan. In a medium bowl, combine cake mix, egg and 1/2 cup water. Beat 2 minutes with an electric mixer on medium speed. Scrape side and bottom of bowl; beat 2 more minutes. Pour batter into prepared pan. Bake 12 to 15 minutes or until a wooden pick inserted in center comes out clean. Cool in pan on a rack. In a medium bowl, beat powdered sugar and cream cheese until smooth. Fold in whipped cream. Spread mixture over cooled cake. Refrigerate. In a medium saucepan, combine Danish dessert and 3 cups water. Cook over medium-high heat, stirring constantly, until mixture boils and thickens. Remove from heat; cool. Stir in strawberries. (If using strawberry glaze, simply stir sliced berries into glaze; do not heat.) Spoon strawberry mixture over cream-cheese mixture. Refrigerate at least 1 hour or up to 2 days before serving. Makes 15 servings.

Barbara's English Trifle; Granny's Banana Cake, page 16; Choco-Orange Cake, page 28.

Ilene's Carrot Ring

Use this bread-like vegetable ring to accompany meat or poultry entrees.

1-1/4 cups grated carrots
1 tablespoon lemon juice
1 tablespoon water
1 egg, beaten
1/2 cup packed brown sugar
1/2 cup vegetable oil

1-1/4 cups all-purpose flour
2 teaspoons baking powder
1/2 teaspoon salt
1-1/2 cups hot cooked broccoli spears or
    cooked peas

Preheat oven to 375F (190C). Generously oil a 1-quart ovenproof ring mold. In a medium bowl, combine carrots, lemon juice, water, egg, brown sugar and oil; beat until blended. In a small bowl, sift together flour, baking powder and salt. Stir into carrot mixture. Pour into oiled ring mold. Place mold in a baking dish; pour boiling water into baking dish until water is halfway up side of mold. Bake 45 to 55 minutes or until a wooden pick inserted in center comes out clean. Cool in mold on a rack 5 minutes; unmold onto a platter. Fill center with hot broccoli spears or peas. Serve immediately. Makes 6 to 8 servings.

Stir-Fry Vegetable Medley   *Photo on page 60.*

Try using other vegetables, such as zucchini, green beans, or whatever is accumulating in your garden.

2 medium carrots
2 celery stalks
1 medium bunch broccoli
About 2 tablespoons vegetable oil
1 medium onion, thinly sliced

1/2 lb. large fresh mushrooms,
    cut in quarters
1/4 cup water
1-1/4 teaspoons salt
1/2 teaspoon sugar

Cut carrots and celery in 3-inch-long julienne strips. Cut broccoli stalks and flowerets in 2'' x 1/2'' pieces. In a wok or large skillet, heat oil over high heat. Add carrots, celery, broccoli and onion. Cook 3 to 4 minutes, stirring quickly and frequently. Add mushrooms, water, salt and sugar. Reduce heat to medium. Cover; cook 5 to 6 more minutes or until vegetables are tender-crisp, stirring occasionally. Makes 8 servings.

Minted Carrots

Be sure to prepare this dish ahead so the mint flavor can penetrate the carrots.

2 lbs. carrots, peeled, sliced
4 teaspoons cornstarch
1/2 cup sugar

1 (6-oz.) can pineapple juice
2 tablespoons butter or margarine
1-1/2 teaspoons dried leaf mint

Place carrots in a large saucepan. Add a small amount of water. Bring to a boil; reduce heat. Cover; simmer about 15 to 20 minutes or until tender. Drain. In a small bowl, combine cornstarch, sugar and pineapple juice; pour over carrots in saucepan. Add butter or margarine. Cook over medium heat, stirring constantly, until sauce is thickened. Stir in mint; cool slightly. Cover; refrigerate at least 2 hours or up to 12 hours. Reheat before serving. Makes 6 to 8 servings.

How to Make Ilene's Carrot Ring

1/Carefully pour batter into an oiled ring mold. Place in a baking dish; pour boiling water into dish until water is halfway up side of mold.

2/Cool, in mold, on a rack 5 minutes; unmold onto a platter. Fill center with hot cooked broccoli. Garnish as desired.

Carrot Cake

The non-carrot-lover's favorite way to eat his veggies!

2 cups sugar
4 eggs
1-1/2 cups vegetable oil
2-1/2 cups all-purpose flour
2 teaspoons baking soda

1 teaspoon salt
2 teaspoons ground cinnamon
3 cups finely grated carrots
1 cup chopped nuts
Cream-Cheese Frosting, see below

Cream-Cheese Frosting:
1/2 cup butter or margarine,
 room temperature
1 (8-oz.) pkg. cream cheese,
 room temperature

1 teaspoon vanilla extract
1 (16-oz.) pkg. powdered sugar
 (4 cups unsifted)

Preheat oven to 350F (175C). Grease a 13'' x 9'' baking pan. In a large bowl, combine sugar, eggs, oil, flour, baking soda, salt, cinnamon and carrots. Using an electric mixer, beat 3 minutes or until blended. Stir in nuts. Pour batter into greased pan. Bake 35 minutes or until a wooden pick inserted in center comes out clean. Cool in pan on a rack. Prepare Cream-Cheese Frosting; spread over cooled cake. Makes 12 to 15 servings.

Cream-Cheese Frosting:
In a large bowl, cream butter or margarine, cream cheese and vanilla. Add powdered sugar; beat until smooth and creamy.

Puffy Fried Vegetables

A golden, soufflé-type coating enhances your choice of vegetables.

Fresh vegetables, see below
1/2 teaspoon salt
1 (8-oz.) can stewed tomatoes or
    1 (8-oz.) can tomato sauce

1/4 teaspoon garlic salt
4 eggs, separated
Vegetable oil for frying

Place vegetable of your choice in a large saucepan. Add a small amount of water and 1/4 teaspoon salt. Cover; heat until water comes to a boil. Reduce heat. If using cauliflower or green beans, continue to cook until tender-crisp. If using spinach, continue to cook only 2 more minutes. *Drain vegetable well;* set aside. In a small saucepan, heat stewed tomatoes or tomato sauce until hot. Stir in garlic salt; cover and keep warm. In a medium bowl, beat egg whites until stiff but not dry. In a large bowl, beat egg yolks and remaining 1/4 teaspoon salt until lemon-colored. Fold beaten egg whites into egg-yolk mixture. In a large skillet, heat about 1/4 inch of oil to 375F (190C). Dip vegetable of your choice into egg mixture — 1 caulifloweret, a spoonful of bean pieces or a small portion of spinach at a time. Carefully place in hot oil; fry 2 to 4 minutes or until golden on all sides, turning as needed. Drain on paper towels. Top vegetables with warm tomato mixture. Serve immediately. Makes 6 servings.

Suggested fresh vegetables:
1 medium head cauliflower, cut in cauliflowerets; or 1 pound green beans, cut in 2- to 3-inch lengths; or 1 large bunch spinach, stems removed, leaves washed and patted dry.

Cranberry-Fruit Salad

Buy plenty of cranberries at Thanksgiving time, then store them in your freezer to use throughout the year.

2 cups fresh or frozen cranberries,
    coarsely ground
1 cup sugar

1/2 pint whipping cream (1 cup), whipped
1 cup seedless green grapes
1/2 cup chopped nuts

In a medium bowl, combine cranberries and sugar. Cover; refrigerate at least 8 hours or up to 24 hours. At serving time, drain and discard juice from cranberries. Fold whipped cream, grapes and nuts into drained cranberries. Makes 6 servings.

Refrigerator Spiced Pickles

Makes a nice crisp snack when you feel like nibbling.

6 cucumbers, sliced 1/4 inch thick
2 white onions, thinly sliced
2 cups white distilled vinegar

2-1/2 cups sugar
2 tablespoons salt
1/2 teaspoon celery seeds

Alternately pack cucumbers and onions tightly into 2 (1-quart) jars. In a medium saucepan, combine vinegar, sugar and salt. Bring to a boil, stirring until sugar is dissolved. Remove from heat; cool. Stir in celery seeds. Pour cooled mixture over cucumbers and onions in jars. Attach lids; refrigerate at least 12 hours or up to 6 weeks. Makes 2 quarts.

Grapefruit-Slush Base

Here's a refreshing fruit cup you can keep on hand in your freezer for months.

1 cup water
1 cup sugar
5 or 6 grapefruit, sectioned,
  including juice (about 4 cups)

1 (20-oz.) can crushed pineapple
1 (10-oz.) pkg. frozen unsweetened
  strawberries, slightly thawed

In a small saucepan, combine water and sugar; stir over medium heat until sugar is dissolved. Remove from heat; cool. Place grapefruit sections and juice in a large bowl. Gently stir in undrained pineapple and strawberries. Add cooled sugar mixture. Divide mixture evenly among 4 (2-cup) freezer containers. Attach lids; freeze until firm or up to 6 months. Makes 8 cups.

To make Grapefruit Slush:
2 cups Grapefruit Slush,
  slightly thawed

2 cups grape juice, orange juice, pineapple
  juice, lemon-lime soda or ginger ale

In a medium bowl, combine Grapefruit Slush with fruit juice, lemon-lime soda or ginger ale. Stir gently. Serve in dessert dishes. Makes 4 servings.

Variation
Substitute 2 (16-ounce) cans grapefruit sections, undrained, for fresh grapefruit.

Arizona Breakfast Grapefruit

Try this tangy fruit cup for breakfast or dessert.

1 cup water
2 cups sugar
1 (3-oz.) pkg. lemon-flavored gelatin

10 to 12 grapefruit, sectioned,
  including juice (about 8 cups)

In a small saucepan, bring water to a boil. Remove from heat; add sugar and gelatin and stir until dissolved. Cool. Place grapefruit sections and juice in a large bowl. Add gelatin mixture; stir to blend. Refrigerate 3 to 4 hours or until well chilled. Use within 2 weeks. To serve, spoon into dessert dishes. Makes about 8 cups.

Variation
If desired, you may spoon this mixture into 4 (2-cup) freezer containers; freeze up to 6 months. To serve, thaw until slushy; spoon into shallow dessert dishes.

Lemon Pot Roast

A new flavor for the humble pot roast.

1 (2-1/2-lb.) boneless beef chuck roast
   or thick beef top round steak
1-1/2 cups water
1/2 cup lemon juice
1 onion, chopped
1 teaspoon salt

1 teaspoon celery salt
1 teaspoon onion salt
1 teaspoon pepper
1/4 teaspoon ground marjoram
1 garlic clove, minced
3 lemon slices, cut in quarters

Put roast in a shallow pan or marinating container. In a medium bowl, combine remaining ingredients. Pour over roast. Cover; refrigerate at least 4 hours or up to 24 hours. Remove roast from marinade; place in a roasting pan. Cover and bake in a 325F (165C) oven 1-1/2 to 2 hours or until tender when pierced with a fork. Makes about 6 servings.

Luscious Lemon Ice Cream

Lemon lovers will delight in this simple, wonderfully refreshing treat.

1-1/2 pints whipping cream (3 cups)
1-1/2 cups sugar

3/4 cup fresh lemon juice (about 4 lemons)
1 tablespoon grated lemon peel

In a medium bowl, combine cream and sugar. Stir until sugar is dissolved. Place mixture in freezer; freeze about 3 hours or until slushy. Stir in lemon juice and lemon peel; beat with an electric mixer until almost smooth. Return to freezer for 2 hours. Beat again; freeze until solid. Use within 2 weeks. Makes about 1 quart.

Fresh Lemonade Syrup

Real "old-fashioned" lemonade is easy to make if you keep a supply of this syrup in the refrigerator.

8 or 9 lemons
2 cups sugar

1 cup water
1/8 teaspoon salt

Cut lemons in half crosswise; juice lemons to equal 1-3/4 cups. Reserve 2 juiced lemon halves; cut in quarters. Put lemon juice in a 1-quart container. In a small saucepan, combine quartered lemon halves, sugar, water and salt. Bring to a boil. Reduce heat; simmer, uncovered, 5 minutes. Remove from heat; cool. Stir cooled sugar mixture into lemon juice. Cover; refrigerate up to 1 month. Makes about 3-1/2 cups.

To make Fresh Lemonade:
1/4 cup Fresh Lemonade Syrup
3/4 cup iced water or carbonated water

Place Fresh Lemonade Syrup in a glass. Add iced water or carbonated water; stir. Serve immediately. Makes 1 serving.

How to Make Orange Cookies

1/Cut unpeeled oranges into chunks; remove seeds. In a processor fitted with a metal blade, process until finely chopped, making about 1-1/2 cups.

2/Drop batter by teaspoons onto greased baking sheets. Bake until edges are golden. Frost warm cookies, then cool completely.

Orange Cookies

For these drop cookies, you really use the whole orange!

**2 medium oranges, unpeeled
  (1-1/2 cups finely chopped)**
3/4 cup vegetable shortening
1-1/4 cups sugar
2 eggs
3-1/2 cups all-purpose flour

1 teaspoon baking powder
1/2 teaspoon salt
1 teaspoon baking soda
1 cup milk
Frosting, see below

Frosting:
1/2 cup finely chopped oranges
2 tablespoons butter or margarine, melted

2 to 3 cups powdered sugar

Preheat oven to 375F (190C). Lightly grease baking sheets. Cut oranges in chunks and remove seeds; place in a food processor fitted with a metal blade. Process until finely chopped; you should have about 1-1/2 cups. Set aside. In a large bowl, cream shortening and sugar. Beat in eggs. Add flour, baking powder, salt, baking soda, milk and 1 cup of the chopped oranges (reserve remaining 1/2 cup chopped oranges for Frosting). Mix well. Drop by teaspoons onto greased baking sheets, spacing cookies 1-1/2 to 2 inches apart. Bake 8 to 9 minutes or until edges of cookies are golden. Remove cookies from baking sheets; transfer to racks. Prepare Frosting; frost cookies while still warm. Cool cookies completely on racks. Makes 72 to 84 cookies.
Frosting:
In a small bowl, combine 1/2 cup reserved chopped oranges, melted butter or margarine and powdered sugar. Stir to blend well.

Choco-Orange Cake   *Photo on page 21.*

Maraschino cherries give this cake its extra-moist texture.

1/4 cup orange juice
3 tablespoons coarsely grated orange peel
1 (18-1/4-oz.) pkg. orange-flavored
   cake mix
1 (4-1/2-oz.) pkg. instant
   chocolate pudding mix
4 eggs

1 cup water
1/4 cup vegetable oil
3/4 cup chopped walnuts
1/2 cup chopped maraschino cherries,
   drained well
Orange Glaze, see below
8 maraschino cherry halves

Orange Glaze:
1-1/2 cups powdered sugar
2 tablespoons orange juice

1 tablespoon lemon juice

Preheat oven to 350F (175C). Generously grease and flour a 10-inch Bundt pan. In a small saucepan, bring orange juice to a boil over high heat. Remove from heat; add orange peel. Set aside to cool. In a large bowl, combine cake mix, pudding mix, eggs, water and oil. Beat with an electric mixer on medium speed 4 minutes, scraping side and bottom of bowl frequently. Stir in cooled orange-juice mixture, walnuts and chopped cherries. Pour batter into prepared pan. Bake 40 to 45 minutes or until a wooden pick inserted in center comes out clean. While cake is baking, prepare Orange Glaze. Cool baked cake in pan on a rack 15 minutes. Turn out cake onto a plate; immediately drizzle with glaze. Cool. Evenly space cherry halves on top of cake. If preparing ahead, tightly wrap cooled cake; freeze up to 3 months. Makes about 12 servings.
Orange Glaze:
In a small bowl, combine powdered sugar, orange juice and lemon juice. Stir until smooth.

Orange Syrup

Here's a refreshing change from maple syrup for your favorite pancakes and waffles.

1-1/4 cups fresh orange juice
   (about 3 oranges)
1 tablespoon grated orange peel

4-1/2 teaspoons cornstarch
1/4 teaspoon salt
1/2 cup sugar

In a small saucepan, combine orange juice, orange peel, cornstarch, salt and sugar. Blend well. Cook over medium-high heat, stirring constantly, until thickened. Serve hot over waffles or pancakes. If preparing ahead, cover; refrigerate up to 1 week. Reheat before serving. Makes 1-1/2 cups.

How to Make Potato Nests

1/Spoon mixture equally into buttered muffin cups. Press over bottoms and up sides of cups.

2/Run a knife around edges of nests; carefully slip out of muffin cups. Serve warm, filled with hot vegetables of your choice.

Potato Nests

These whimsical "baskets" will add a touch of class to your next brunch or luncheon — and you can make them up to 24 hours ahead.

About 4 cups cold water
3 medium potatoes
1/4 cup minced onion
1/4 cup shredded Swiss cheese (1 oz.)
1 egg yolk
1/4 teaspoon salt

1/4 teaspoon pepper
1/4 teaspoon paprika
About 3 cups hot cooked vegetables of
   your choice — green peas and baby
   onions, creamed green peas,
   creamed mushrooms or creamed carrots

Preheat oven to 350F (175C). Butter 12 muffin cups; set aside. Pour cold water into a large bowl. Peel potatoes; grate into water. Drain; squeeze out excess moisture. In a medium bowl, combine drained potatoes, onion, cheese, egg yolk, salt, pepper and paprika. Spoon mixture equally into buttered muffin cups. Press over bottoms and up sides of cups. Bake 30 to 35 minutes or until sides are golden brown. Cool slightly in pans. Run a knife around edges of nests; carefully slip out of muffin cups. Serve warm, filled with hot vegetables of your choice. If prepared ahead, cool nests completely on racks. Wrap tightly; refrigerate up to 24 hours. To reheat, place nests, upside down, on a baking sheet. Heat in a 400F (205C) oven, 5 minutes. Makes 12 servings.

Idaho Stuffed Spudskins

A topping of cheesy creamed crab turns a plain baked potato into an elegant entree.

6 large baking potatoes
2 tablespoons butter or margarine, melted

Cheesy Crab Sauce, see below

Cheesy Crab Sauce:
3 tablespoons butter or margarine
3 tablespoons all-purpose flour
1-1/2 cups milk

3 cups shredded Muenster cheese (12 oz.)
3/4 lb. fresh or frozen crabmeat, thawed if frozen

Scrub potatoes well; pierce each with a fork in several places. Place directly on oven rack. Bake in a 400F (205C) oven, 1 hour or until tender when pierced with a fork. Cut potatoes in half lengthwise. Scoop out centers, leaving a 1/4-inch-thick shell. Save centers for other uses, such as fried potatoes or Norwegian Lefse, page 141. Increase oven temperature to 500F (260C). Place potato shells on a baking sheet; brush with melted butter or margarine. Bake 20 minutes or until edges are browned. While shells are baking, prepare Cheesy Crab Sauce. Spoon hot sauce equally into hot potato shells. Makes 6 servings.

Cheesy Crab Sauce:
In a medium saucepan, melt butter or margarine over low heat. Stir in flour until blended. Cook, stirring 1 minute. Slowly add milk, stirring with a whisk until smooth. Continue to cook and stir until sauce is bubbly and thickened. Remove from heat. Add cheese and crabmeat; stir until cheese is melted. Keep hot until ready to serve.

Rose's Rhubarb Cake

This cake frosts itself and is so delicious.

1-1/4-lbs. rhubarb, cubed (5 cups)
1 cup sugar
1 (3-oz.) pkg. strawberry-flavored gelatin

3 cups miniature marshmallows
1 (18-1/4-oz.) pkg. white-cake mix,
**   prepared according to package directions**

Preheat oven to 350F (175C). Spread rhubarb over bottom of an ungreased 13'' x 9'' baking dish. Sprinkle with sugar and gelatin. Arrange marshmallows evenly on top. Pour prepared cake batter over mixture in baking dish. Bake 50 to 55 minutes or until a wooden pick inserted in center comes out clean. Turn out cake onto a platter while still warm. Makes 12 to 15 servings.

Perfect Pumpkin Pie

The Bluebird Restaurant in northern Utah made this pumpkin pie famous for miles around.

1 (29-oz.) can solid-pack pumpkin
   (*not* pumpkin-pie mix) or
   3 cups mashed cooked pumpkin
1-1/2 cups granulated sugar
1/4 cup packed dark-brown sugar
1/3 cup all-purpose flour
1 teaspoon salt
1 teaspoon ground cinnamon
3/4 teaspoon ground ginger

1/2 teaspoon ground allspice
1/8 teaspoon ground cloves
Dash of ground nutmeg
2 eggs
1 (12-oz.) can evaporated milk
1 tablespoon butter or margarine
2 (8-inch) baked pastry shells
1/2 pint whipping cream (1 cup),
   whipped, sweetened

In the top of a double boiler, combine pumpkin, sugars, flour, salt, cinnamon, ginger, allspice, cloves and nutmeg. Beat with an electric mixer until blended. Beat in eggs and evaporated milk until blended. Cook over simmering water, stirring, until mixture thickens and loses its gloss. Remove from heat; stir in butter or margarine. Cool 5 minutes. Spoon mixture into pastry shells. Refrigerate several hours or until firm, or up to 24 hours. Serve with whipped cream. Makes 2 pies, 6 to 8 servings each.

Raisin-Almond Spinach Salad

A nice accompaniment for seafood or poultry dishes.

Sweet Russian Dressing, see below
1 lb. spinach, stems removed, leaves washed
   and torn in pieces

Sweet Russian Dressing:
1/4 cup sugar
1/4 cup white-wine vinegar or rice vinegar

1 cup shredded red cabbage
1/4 cup raisins
3 tablespoons slivered almonds, toasted

1/4 cup vegetable oil
1/4 cup ketchup

Prepare Sweet Russian Dressing; refrigerate. In a large bowl, toss together spinach, cabbage and raisins. Add dressing; toss until dressing is evenly distributed. Sprinkle salad with toasted almonds; serve immediately. Makes 6 to 8 servings.

Sweet Russian Dressing:
In a small bowl, combine sugar, vinegar, oil and ketchup. Beat to blend well; cover and refrigerate. Makes about 1 cup.

Fried Zucchini

A restaurant specialty that you can easily make at home.

Garlic Dip, see below
1/4 cup all-purpose flour
1/4 teaspoon salt
1/4 teaspoon seasoned salt
1/8 teaspoon pepper
1/8 teaspoon garlic powder

2 eggs
2 tablespoons lemon juice
1 cup fine cracker crumbs or dry bread crumbs
Vegetable oil for frying
3 medium zucchini, cut diagonally in
   1/4-inch-thick slices

Garlic Dip:
1/2 cup mayonnaise
1/2 cup buttermilk
1 teaspoon dried parsley flakes

1 teaspoon instant minced onion
1/4 teaspoon salt
Pinch of garlic powder

Prepare Garlic Dip; refrigerate. In a shallow dish, combine flour, salt, seasoned salt, pepper and garlic powder. In a small bowl, lightly beat together eggs and lemon juice. Put crumbs in another small bowl. In a small skillet, heat 1/2 inch of oil to 375F (190C). Dip zucchini slices in flour mixture, then in egg mixture, then in crumbs. Lower zucchini, a few pieces at a time, into hot oil; fry 1 to 2 minutes or until golden. Drain on paper towels. Serve hot with Garlic Dip. Makes 4 servings.

Garlic Dip:
In a small bowl, combine mayonnaise, buttermilk, parsley flakes, instant minced onion, salt and garlic powder. Cover and refrigerate.

Zucchini Bake

A wonderful side dish to serve with roast beef.

4 cups sliced zucchini
   (1/4-inch-thick slices)
3 tablespoons water
1 teaspoon salt
3 tablespoons butter or margarine
3/4 cup chopped onion
1 large green bell pepper, diced

1 (8-oz.) can water chestnuts,
   drained, sliced
Black pepper to taste
1-1/4 cups shredded Cheddar cheese
   (5 oz.)
1/4 teaspoon paprika

Butter an 11'' x 7'' baking dish. Place zucchini in a medium saucepan; add 3 tablespoons water and salt. Bring to a boil; reduce heat. Cover; steam 8 to 12 minutes or until tender-crisp. Drain well; place in buttered dish. In a medium skillet, melt butter or margarine. Add onion, bell pepper and water chestnuts; sauté until onion is tender but not browned. Stir in black pepper. Spoon sautéed vegetables over zucchini. Cover with cheese; sprinkle with paprika. Bake, uncovered, in a 350F (175C) oven, 20 minutes or until cheese is melted. Makes 6 to 8 servings.

A-Z Bread

This accommodating recipe provides a delicious use for everything from surplus apples to overabundant zucchini.

3 cups all-purpose flour
1 tablespoon ground cinnamon
1 teaspoon baking soda
1 teaspoon salt
1/2 teaspoon baking powder
3 eggs
2 cups packed brown sugar,
granulated sugar or a combination

2/3 cup vegetable oil
2 cups cooked, uncooked or drained
canned fruits or vegetables, see below
1 tablespoon vanilla extract
1 cup chopped walnuts or pecans
1 cup chopped raisins or dates, if desired

Preheat oven to 325F (165C). Lightly grease and flour 2 (8-1/2'' x 4-1/2'') loaf pans. In a medium bowl, stir together flour, cinnamon, baking soda, salt and baking powder; set aside. In a large bowl, beat eggs; stir in sugar and oil. Stir in fruits or vegetables and vanilla. Stir in flour mixture and nuts; stir in raisins or dates, if desired. Pour batter into prepared pans. Bake 50 to 60 minutes or until a wooden pick inserted in center comes out clean. Cool in pans on a rack 5 minutes. Remove from pans, cool completely on rack. If preparing ahead, wrap cooled loaves airtight. Refrigerate up to 4 days or freeze up to 2 months. Makes 2 loaves.

Suggested fruits and vegetables:
Chopped or grated uncooked apples; applesauce; chopped uncooked or mashed cooked apricots; mashed avocados; mashed bananas; mashed or pureed strawberries, blackberries, raspberries or blueberries; shredded fresh or mashed cooked carrots; pitted, chopped sweet cherries; ground fresh or frozen cranberries; finely chopped or pureed nectarines; ground oranges; finely chopped or pureed uncooked fresh or canned peaches; pureed uncooked fresh or canned pears; crushed pineapple; canned or mashed cooked pumpkin; mashed cooked rhubarb; grated uncooked fresh or mashed cooked zucchini.

Seafood Creole Gumbo

Ready to serve in less than an hour.

1/4 cup butter or margarine
3 tablespoons all-purpose flour
1 garlic clove, minced
2 onions, sliced
1/2 green bell pepper, cut in thin strips
1 lb. okra, sliced
6 large fresh tomatoes or
   2 (16-oz.) cans tomatoes

2 cups water
1 (14-1/2-oz.) can chicken broth
1 teaspoon salt
1 tablespoon Worcestershire sauce
2 lbs. uncooked shrimp, shelled, deveined
Hot cooked rice

In a large, heavy skillet, melt butter or margarine over low heat. Stir in flour; cook, stirring constantly, until browned. Stir in garlic, onions, bell pepper and okra. Continue to cook slowly until vegetables are tender. Chop fresh or canned tomatoes; add chopped tomatoes and their juice to skillet. Then add water, broth, salt and Worcestershire sauce. Cover; simmer 20 minutes or until slightly thickened. Add shrimp; continue to cook 5 more minutes or just until shrimp turn pink. To serve, spoon a mound of rice into shallow plates; top with gumbo. Makes 8 servings.

Grandma Child's Chunky Chili Sauce

Grandma was famous for this sauce — and now the compliments can be yours!

24 large tomatoes (10 to 12 lbs.),
   diced
5 green bell peppers, diced
2 hot or mild long green chilies,
   seeded, diced
3 large onions, finely diced
1 cup packed brown sugar
1 cup granulated sugar

3 tablespoons salt
1 cup cider vinegar
1 teaspoon whole allspice
1 teaspoon mustard seeds
1 teaspoon celery seeds
1 (2-inch) cinnamon stick
1 teaspoon whole cloves
1 (32-oz.) bottle ketchup

Put tomatoes in a large Dutch oven. Stir in bell peppers, chilies, onions, sugars, salt and vinegar. Cut a 6-inch square of cheesecloth; spoon allspice, mustard seeds, celery seeds, cinnamon stick and cloves onto cloth. Bring cloth up around spices; tie with a piece of thread. Add to tomato mixture. Bring mixture to a boil, stirring constantly. Reduce heat. Simmer, uncovered, 2 to 3 hours, stirring occasionally to prevent sticking. Add ketchup; continue to cook 1 more hour or until mixture is as thick as desired. Remove wrapped spices; ladle hot sauce into 1-pint jars, leaving 1/4 inch headspace. Wipe rims of jars with a clean, damp cloth; attach lids. Process 15 minutes in a boiling water bath, or freeze up to 8 months. Makes 12 to 13 pints.

Variation
Smooth Chili Sauce: If you prefer a smoother chili sauce, puree tomatoes in a food processor fitted with a metal blade or in a blender before cooking.

How to Make Homemade Fruit Ice Cream

1/Pour blended fruit mixture into an ice-cream canister. Stir in enough milk to bring mixture to within 1-1/2 inches of top of container.

2/Freeze according to manufacturer's directions. When firm, form scoops and place on a tray; freeze until ready to serve. Garnish with fresh fruit, if desired.

Homemade Fruit Ice Cream

Favorite fruit selections for this recipe include peaches, strawberries and raspberries.

4 eggs
3 cups sugar
4 cups fresh fruit, such as sliced peaches,
strawberries or raspberries

1/2 cup fresh lemon juice
1/2 teaspoon salt
1 qt. whipping cream (4 cups)
About 1 pint milk (2 cups)

In a blender or a food processor fitted with a metal blade, combine eggs, sugar, fruit, lemon juice and salt. Process about 20 seconds or until blended and smooth; stir in cream. Pour into an ice-cream freezer container. Stir in enough milk to bring mixture to within 1-1/2 inches of top of container. Freeze according to manufacturer's directions. Makes about 4 quarts.

Fruit Dips & Toppers

Either of these smooth, creamy dip/toppings will enhance any fresh fruit.

Citrus-Creme Topping or Yogurt Fluff,
  see below

Assorted fresh fruits, see below

Citrus-Creme Topping:
1 (8-oz.) pkg. cream cheese,
  room temperature
1 (7-oz.) jar marshmallow creme

2 to 3 tablespoons fresh lime juice or
  1 to 2 tablespoons frozen orange
  juice concentrate, thawed

Yogurt Fluff:
1 (8-oz.) carton frozen whipped topping,
  thawed

1 (6- or 8-oz.) carton raspberry or
  other fruit-flavored yogurt

Prepare Citrus-Creme Topping or Yogurt Fluff. Cover; refrigerate until well chilled. Serve as a topping or a dip for fresh fruits of your choice.
Citrus Creme Topping:
In a medium bowl, combine cream cheese, marshmallow creme and lime juice or orange juice concentrate. Beat with an electric mixer until blended. Cover; refrigerate. Makes about 1-1/2 cups.
Yogurt Fluff:
In a medium bowl, combine whipped topping and yogurt. Cover; refrigerate. Makes about 2-1/2 cups.

Suggested fresh fruits:
Choose from banana slices, kiwifruit slices, mango slices or chunks, melon cubes or wedges, papaya slices, peach or nectarine slices, pear slices, whole strawberries or other berries.

Dill Dip   *Photo on page 78.*

Complements ordinary carrot sticks or a fancy crudité arrangement.

1 cup mayonnaise
1/2 pint dairy sour cream (1 cup)
1 tablespoon instant minced onion
1 tablespoon dried parsley flakes

1 teaspoon dried dill weed
1 teaspoon Bon Appetit seasoning
Assorted uncooked vegetables, see below
Dill sprig, optional

In a medium bowl, combine mayonnaise, sour cream, instant minced onion, parsley flakes, dill weed and Bon Appetit. Cover; refrigerate at least 2 hours or up to 2 days before serving. Garnish with a dill sprig, if desired. Serve with assorted vegetables. Makes about 2 cups.

Suggested vegetables:
Choose from broccoli or cauliflower flowerets, carrot sticks, celery sticks, jícama strips, green or red bell pepper strips, cherry tomatoes, turnip or sweet potato slices, zucchini or crookneck squash slices.

CHAPTER TWO

Big-Batch

Many recipes are well-suited to "Big-Batch" cookery. Long-simmered sauces such as Spaghetti Sauce Supreme can easily be cooked in large quantities, then frozen for use in many meals. Quantity cooking is also appropriate for most casseroles. If you're preparing a favorite that requires a little extra effort to assemble, it makes good sense to fix two or three at a time and freeze the extras for fuss-free meals. And of course, big-batch recipes are ideal choices when you're looking for ways to use abundant fresh fruits and vegetables in season (you'll find more ideas in Chapter 1). Our Frozen Fruit Combo, for example, puts early autumn's peaches and pears to delicious use. With several batches of this frosty treat on hand, you can enjoy a fresh-fruit dessert even in midwinter.

Frozen Fruit-Punch Base

A refreshing crowd-pleaser.

6 cups water
4 cups sugar
1 (46-oz.) can pineapple juice

1/2 cup fresh lemon juice
2 cups orange juice
5 large bananas, mashed (2-1/2 cups)

In a large saucepan, combine water and sugar. Bring to a boil, stirring until sugar is dissolved. Remove from heat; cool. Stir in pineapple juice, lemon juice, orange juice and bananas. Pour 6 cups of the mixture into each of 3 (1/2-gallon) freezer containers. Attach lids; freeze up to 8 months. Makes 3 containers, each containing enough base for 40 servings.

To make Fruit Punch:
1 container Frozen Fruit-Punch Base, thawed 1 hour
1 cup frozen strawberries or raspberries, if desired, thawed just enough to break apart easily

1 to 1-1/2 liters lemon-lime soda, well chilled

Place Frozen Fruit-Punch Base in a large punch bowl; break up slightly with a spoon. Add strawberries or raspberries, if desired. Gently stir in lemon-lime soda. Makes about 40 servings.

Do-Ahead Tomato-Vegetable Soup

This recipe won a cooking contest we recently judged.

1-1/2 cups pearl barley
5 cups water
15 lbs. tomatoes (about 45 medium)
2 green bell peppers, diced
2 onions, chopped

1/2 cup chopped fresh parsley
8 to 10 carrots, peeled and sliced or diced
6 celery stalks, sliced
2/3 cup sugar
3 tablespoons salt

Place barley and water in a large saucepan. Cover and cook over low heat 1 hour or until tender. Remove pan from heat; drain, if necessary. While barley is cooking, peel tomatoes and puree in a blender or a food processor fitted with a metal blade. Pour puree into a large canning kettle or Dutch oven; bring to a boil. Reduce heat, and simmer, uncovered, 30 minutes, stirring occasionally to prevent sticking. In another large saucepan, combine bell peppers, onions, parsley, carrots and celery. Add a small amount of water. Bring to boil; reduce heat, cover and simmer 15 minutes or until vegetables are tender. Add cooked, drained barley and undrained cooked vegetables to tomato puree. Stir in sugar and salt. Bring to a boil; reduce heat and simmer, uncovered, 30 minutes. Serve hot. If preparing ahead, pour soup into large-mouth 1-quart jars, leaving 1/2 inch headspace. Wipe rims of jars with a clean, damp cloth; attach lids. Process in a pressure cooker according to manufacturer's directions 10 minutes at 10 pounds pressure or as adjusted for altitude. Or freeze up to 6 months. Makes about 8 quarts, 3 or 4 servings per quart.

Variation
Add cooked ground beef or chicken when serving soup, if desired.

Do-Ahead Frozen Fruit Salads

These creamy little salads are great to have on hand in the freezer for drop-in guests.

1 qt. dairy sour cream (4 cups)	1 (20-oz.) can crushed pineapple, drained
1/4 cup lemon juice	1/3 cup maraschino cherries, drained, halved
1-1/2 cups sugar	1 cup chopped nuts
1/4 teaspoon salt	Lettuce leaves
4 or 5 large bananas, diced	

Line 24 muffin cups with paper baking cups. In a large bowl, combine sour cream, lemon juice, sugar and salt. Stir in bananas, pineapple, cherries and nuts. Spoon fruit mixture into paper-lined muffin cups. Freeze 2 hours or until frozen solid. Remove from muffin cups; store in an airtight container in freezer up to 3 months. At serving time, peel off paper baking cups. Place salads on lettuce leaves. Makes about 24 servings.

Mini-Chimis

A small version of an all-time Arizona favorite. Serve with Guacamole, page 13, and Eldora's Salsa, opposite.

2-1/2 to 3 lbs. beef roast,	2 tablespoons all-purpose flour
pork roast or a combination	1 teaspoon salt
(about 4 cups shredded cooked meat)	1/2 teaspoon ground cumin
1 tablespoon vegetable shortening	1-1/4 cups meat juices
1 cup diced onions	(reserved from cooking roast)
1 (4-oz.) can diced green chilies	Vegetable oil for deep-frying
1 (7-oz.) can green-chili salsa	2 (16-oz.) pkgs. won-ton skins
1/4 teaspoon garlic powder	

Preheat oven to 325F (165C). Place roast in a large roasting pan or Dutch oven. Cover with a tight-fitting lid. Roast about 3 hours or until meat is tender and shreds easily. Skim and discard fat from meat cooking juices; reserve 1-1/4 cups juices. Cool meat slightly; remove bones and fat. Shred meat with 2 forks; set aside. In a large skillet, melt shortening. Add onions and chilies; sauté 5 to 6 minutes or until onions are tender but not browned. Stir in green-chili salsa, garlic powder, flour, salt and cumin. Cook 2 minutes over medium-low heat. Stir in reserved meat juices and shredded meat. Cook 5 minutes or until thick, stirring constantly. Remove from heat; cool. In a large skillet, heat 2 inches of oil to 375F (190C) or until a 1-inch bread cube turns golden brown in about 50 seconds. Place 1 heaping teaspoon of the meat mixture in lower corner of each won-ton skin. Fold point of won-ton skin up over filling, then fold side corners in. Moisten top corner with water and roll skin into a cylinder. Repeat with remaining meat and filling. Lower several rolls at a time into hot oil. Fry 3 to 4 minutes or until golden brown, turning if necessary to brown evenly. Drain on paper towels. If preparing ahead, cool, then arrange in a single layer in freezer containers. Cover tightly and freeze up to 3 months. To serve, thaw and place in a single layer on large baking sheets. Preheat oven to 375F (190C); bake rolls 10 to 15 minutes or until crisp, turning once. Makes 120 chimis.

Variation
If using leftover meat, you can use 1-1/4 cups leftover gravy in place of meat cooking juices. Omit the flour.

How to Make Eldora's Salsa

1/Using plastic or rubber gloves, cut chilies in half lengthwise. Scrape out seeds, then dice chilies.

2/Freeze or can salsa in a water bath. Serve with tortilla chips.

Eldora's Salsa

This lively salsa adds zest to all your favorite Mexican dishes. It's a great way to use up your garden tomatoes.

8 hot long yellow chilies
3 jalapeño peppers, seeded, diced
24 medium tomatoes (about 8 lbs.), peeled and pureed or chopped
5 onions, diced
6 green bell peppers, diced
2 garlic cloves, minced
2 tablespoons salt
3 tablespoons sugar
2 tablespoons white distilled vinegar

Using plastic or rubber gloves, cut chilies in half lengthwise; scrape out seeds and dice. In a large Dutch oven, combine tomatoes, onions, bell peppers, diced chilies, diced jalapeno peppers, garlic, salt, sugar and vinegar. Bring mixture to a boil. Reduce heat; simmer, uncovered, 3 to 4 hours or until mixture is thickened. Ladle into 1-pint jars, leaving 1/2 inch headspace. Wipe rims of jars with a clean, damp cloth, then attach lids. Process 45 minutes in a boiling water bath, or freeze up to 8 months. Makes 6 to 7 pints.

Miniature Egg Rolls

Make your choice of fillings—or double the amount of won-ton skins and make both fillings.

Pork or Chicken Filling, see below
Sweet & Sour Sauce, see below

Vegetable oil for deep-frying
2 (16-oz.) pkgs. won-ton skins

Pork Filling:
1 lb. bulk pork sausage
1 cup finely diced celery
1 bunch green onions, finely chopped
4 to 5 cups fresh bean sprouts
1/2 head Chinese cabbage or bok choy, chopped
1 cup finely chopped fresh mushrooms

1 (8-oz.) can water chestnuts, drained, chopped
1 to 2 teaspoons grated fresh gingerroot
1 teaspoon sesame oil
1 tablespoon soy sauce
3 tablespoons water
3 tablespoons cornstarch

Chicken Filling:
1 (4- to 5-lb.) chicken
1 large onion, finely chopped
1/2 bunch celery, finely chopped
5 cups fresh bean sprouts

2 (8-oz.) cans water chestnuts, drained, chopped
1-1/2 teaspoons grated fresh gingerroot
3 tablespoons soy sauce

Sweet & Sour Sauce:
2-1/2 cups pineapple juice
1/4 cup cornstarch
1/4 cup white, distilled vinegar

2 tablespoons soy sauce
2/3 cup packed brown sugar
1/2 cup ketchup

Prepare filling of your choice; set aside. Prepare Sweet & Sour Sauce; keep warm. In a heavy skillet, heat 1-1/2 inches of oil to 375F (190C) or until a 1-inch bread cube turns golden brown in about 50 seconds. Put 1 teaspoon of filling in lower corner of each won-ton skin. Fold bottom point of won-ton skin up over filling, then fold both side corners in. Moisten top corner with water and roll skin into a cylinder. Repeat with remaining meat and filling. Lower several rolls at a time into hot oil; fry 3 to 4 minutes or until golden brown, turning to brown evenly. Drain on paper towels. If preparing ahead, cool, then arrange in a single layer in freezer containers. Cover tightly; freeze up to 3 months. To serve, thaw in refrigerator several hours. Arrange in a single layer on baking sheets. Preheat oven to 375F (190C); bake 10 to 15 minutes or until egg rolls are crisp, turning once. Serve hot with Sweet & Sour Sauce. Makes 120 miniature egg rolls.

Pork Filling:
Crumble sausage into a large skillet or wok. Cook, stirring, until browned. Drain off fat. Add celery, green onions, bean sprouts, Chinese cabbage or bok choy, mushrooms and water chestnuts. Continue to cook, stirring often, until celery is tender-crisp. Meanwhile, in a small bowl, combine gingerroot, sesame oil, soy sauce, water and cornstarch. Stir until smooth. Add to vegetable mixture and continue to cook until mixture is thickened. Cool filling slightly before using.

Chicken Filling:
Place chicken in a Dutch oven; cover with water. Bring to a boil. Reduce heat, cover and simmer 2 to 3 hours or until no longer pink when slashed. Remove chicken from broth; reserve 1/2 cup broth. Cool slightly. Remove and discard skin and bones from chicken; finely chop meat. Place reserved broth in a medium skillet. Add onion and celery; cook 2 to 3 minutes or until tender-crisp. Stir in chopped chicken, bean sprouts, water chestnuts, gingerroot and soy sauce until combined. Cool filling slightly before using.

Sweet & Sour Sauce:
In a medium saucepan, combine pineapple juice and cornstarch. Stir in vinegar, soy sauce, brown sugar and ketchup. Cook over medium heat, stirring occasionally, about 10 minutes or until thickened.

How to Make Chicken Kiev

1/Place chicken breast between two sheets plastic wrap on a flat surface. With flat side of meat mallet, pound chicken until 1/4 inch thick.

2/Wrap flattened chicken around chilled butter balls, tuck in chicken sides and roll up to cover butter completely.

Chicken Kiev

Well worth the effort! Be sure to use butter for the filling — margarine won't work in this recipe.

1 cup butter, room temperature
2 tablespoons finely chopped fresh parsley
2 teaspoons chopped fresh chives
1/2 teaspoon dried leaf tarragon, crushed
2 garlic cloves, minced
1 teaspoon salt
1/4 teaspoon pepper

6 large whole chicken breasts, split, skinned, boned
2/3 cup all-purpose flour
2 eggs, slightly beaten
1/4 cup milk
1 cup fine dry bread crumbs
Vegetable oil for deep-frying

In a medium bowl, combine butter, parsley, chives, tarragon, garlic, salt and pepper. Mix well. Line a baking sheet with wax paper. Drop butter mixture onto wax paper in 12 balls. Place in freezer 15 to 20 minutes. Meanwhile, place each piece of chicken between 2 sheets of plastic wrap. Pound with a flat-surfaced meat mallet until 1/4 inch thick, being careful not to tear meat. Place 1 frozen butter ball in center of each piece of chicken. Wrap chicken around butter, making sure butter is completely enclosed. Put flour in a small bowl. In another small bowl, mix eggs and milk. Put bread crumbs in a third small bowl. Roll each chicken piece first in flour, then in egg mixture, then in bread crumbs. Refrigerate at least 1 hour. If preparing ahead, place rolled-up breaded chicken in an airtight container; freeze up to 3 months. To cook, thaw frozen kiev in refrigerator before deep-frying. Heat about 3 inches of oil in a deep-fryer to 375F (190C) or until a 1-inch bread cube turns golden brown in 50 seconds. Lower chicken pieces into hot oil, a few at a time. Fry 8 minutes or until chicken is deep golden brown and no longer pink when slashed. When testing for doneness, be careful not to cut all the way through to filling. Drain on paper towels; serve hot. Makes 12 servings.

Chicken Supreme Casserole

This casserole can also be made with leftover turkey; just substitute turkey stock for the chicken broth (or use canned chicken broth).

1 (4- to 5-lb.) chicken
1 carrot, trimmed
1 onion, cut in quarters
1-1/2 teaspoons salt

1 bay leaf
Dressing, see below
Supreme Sauce, see below
1 cup fine dry bread crumbs

Dressing:
1 (1-1/2-lb.) loaf day-old bread,
    cubed (16 cups)
3/4 cup butter or margarine
2 medium onions, finely chopped
2 cups chopped celery
1 teaspoon salt

1/2 teaspoon pepper
1-1/2 teaspoons ground sage
1 cup chicken broth (reserved
    from cooking chicken)
1 egg, beaten

Supreme Sauce:
1/2 cup butter or margarine
1/2 cup all-purpose flour
3/4 teaspoon salt
4 cups chicken broth (reserved
    from cooking chicken)

1 cup milk
4 eggs, beaten

Place chicken in a large kettle or Dutch oven; add enough water to cover. Add carrot, onion, salt and bay leaf. Bring to a boil. Reduce heat, cover, and simmer 2 to 3 hours or until meat near thighbone is no longer pink when slashed. Remove chicken from broth. Remove and discard skin and bones. Cut meat into bite-size pieces; set aside. Strain broth, discarding vegetables. Reserve 5 cups of broth to use in Dressing and Supreme Sauce. Preheat oven to 350F (175C). Butter 3 (1-1/2-quart) casserole dishes. Prepare Dressing; divide evenly among buttered dishes. Prepare Supreme Sauce. Using 1/2 of sauce, pour evenly over Dressing in casseroles. Top evenly with chicken and remaining sauce. Sprinkle bread crumbs over top of each casserole. If preparing ahead, cover unbaked casseroles tightly with foil; freeze up to 3 months. Bake, uncovered, 40 to 50 minutes (50 to 60 minutes if frozen) or until heated through. Makes 3 casseroles, 6 servings each.

Dressing:
Place bread cubes in a large bowl or roasting pan. In a medium skillet, melt butter or margarine. Add onions and celery; sauté until onions are tender but not browned. Remove from heat; add salt, pepper, sage and 1 cup reserved broth. Stir a little of the broth mixture into beaten egg; stir egg mixture back into skillet. Pour mixture over bread cubes, stirring to coat completely.

Supreme Sauce:
In a large skillet, melt butter or margarine over low heat. Stir in flour and salt until blended. Cook, stirring, about 1 minute. Slowly add 4 cups reserved broth, stirring with a whisk until smooth. Stir in milk and increase heat to medium. Continue to cook, stirring constantly, until bubbly and thickened. Stir a little of the sauce into beaten eggs, then stir egg mixture back into skillet. Continue to cook and stir until sauce is thickened.

Doubly Delicious Layered Tamale Bake

Chopped green onions, black olives and a dollop of sour cream are nice garnishes for this casserole.

3 lbs. lean ground beef
1 large onion, chopped
2 garlic cloves, minced
3 to 4 tablespoons chili powder
3 (15-oz.) cans tomato sauce
1 teaspoon sugar
2 teaspoons salt
1 (6-oz.) can pitted black olives,
    drained, sliced

1 (7-oz.) can diced green chilies
Vegetable oil for frying
24 (4-1/2- to 5-inch) corn tortillas
24 oz. small-curd cottage cheese (3 cups)
2 eggs
1 lb. Monterey Jack cheese, sliced
2 cups shredded Cheddar cheese (8 oz.)

Crumble beef into a large Dutch oven. Add onion and garlic. Cook, stirring, until meat is browned. Stir in chili powder, tomato sauce, sugar, salt, olives and chilies. Reduce heat; simmer, uncovered, 15 to 20 minutes. Set aside. In a small skillet, heat 1/4 inch of oil to 375F (190C). Lower each tortilla into hot oil; fry 10 to 15 seconds or just until softened but not browned. Drain on paper towels; cut softened tortillas in quarters. Set aside. In a large bowl, beat cottage cheese and eggs together. Set aside. Preheat oven to 350F (175C). Divide 1/3 of the meat mixture equally between 2 (13'' x 9'') baking dishes. Top meat mixture in each dish with 1/4 of the Monterey Jack cheese slices, 1/4 of the cottage-cheese mixture and 1/4 of the quartered tortillas. Repeat layers. Finish each dish with 1 more layer of meat mixture. Top with Cheddar cheese. If preparing ahead, cover unbaked tamale bakes tightly with foil; freeze up to 3 months. To serve, bake, uncovered, 30 to 45 minutes (50 to 60 minutes if frozen) or until heated through. Makes 2 casseroles, 8 servings each.

Spaghetti Sauce Supreme

For every generation this recipe is passed down, it just seems to improve.

2 lbs. sweet Italian sausage,
    casings removed
1 lb. lean ground beef
3 qts. home-canned tomatoes or
    3 (29-oz.) cans tomatoes
2 (12-oz.) cans tomato paste
5 (8-oz.) cans tomato sauce

2 teaspoons dried leaf basil, crushed
2 teaspoons dried parsley flakes, crushed
1 tablespoon freshly grated Romano cheese
1/2 teaspoon garlic powder
1/2 teaspoon pepper
1 lb. pork neck bones
Salt to taste

Crumble sausage and beef into a Dutch oven. Cook over medium-high heat, stirring occasionally, until no longer pink. Drain off fat. Crush tomatoes, then add crushed tomatoes and their juice, tomato paste and tomato sauce to meat in Dutch oven. Add basil, parsley, cheese, garlic powder, pepper and pork bones; stir to distribute. Bring mixture to a boil. Reduce heat, cover; simmer 1 to 3 hours or until mixture is thickened and partially reduced. (Sauce made from home-canned tomatoes generally takes longer to thicken than sauce made with commercially canned tomatoes.) Lift out pork bones; cool slightly. Remove meat from bones; discard bones. Return meat to sauce. Season sauce with salt. If preparing ahead, cool; pour into freezer containers, leaving 1/2 inch headspace. Attach lids; freeze up to 6 months. Serve sauce over spaghetti, or use in your favorite Italian recipes. Makes about 4-1/2 quarts.

Tortilla Basket Salads for a Crowd

Prepare the tortilla baskets ahead; at serving time, just reheat and serve with assorted condiments.

1 (3- to 4-lb.) boneless pork loin or
   butt roast
2 garlic cloves, minced
3/4 teaspoon dried leaf oregano, crushed
1 tablespoon ground cumin
1 (15-oz.) can tomato sauce
1 (10-1/2 oz.) can condensed chicken broth
4 cups water

1 teaspoon salt
2 medium onions, chopped
2 (4-oz.) cans diced green chilies
6 drops hot-pepper sauce
3 cups dried pinto beans, rinsed, sorted,
   soaked overnight
24 Tortilla Baskets, see below
Condiments, see below

Tortilla Baskets:
24 (8- to 10-inch) flour tortillas
Vegetable oil for deep-frying

Condiments:
Shredded iceberg lettuce
Diced tomatoes
Chopped green onions
Shredded Cheddar cheese

Guacamole, page 13
Dairy sour cream
Sliced black olives
Eldora's Salsa, page 41

Trim and discard excess fat from pork roast; cut meat into large pieces. Place meat pieces, garlic, oregano, cumin, tomato sauce, broth, 4 cups water, salt, onions, chilies and hot-pepper sauce in a large Dutch oven. Bring to a boil; reduce heat. Cover; simmer 1 hour. Stir in beans; simmer, covered, for 3-1/2 hours or until meat and beans are tender. Stir and turn meat over occasionally, adding more water as needed. When meat is tender, remove pan from heat. Lift out meat; cool slightly. Shred cooked meat, using 2 forks; stir shredded meat into bean mixture. If preparing ahead, cool and spoon into 6 (1-pint) containers, leaving 1/2 inch headspace. Attach lids; freeze up to 6 months. Thaw in refrigerator overnight. To serve, make Tortilla Baskets and heat meat mixture. Place lettuce into each Tortilla Basket. Spoon 1/2 to 2/3 cup heated meat mixture over lettuce; add other condiments as desired. Makes 24 servings.

Tortilla Baskets:
In a deep 3- to 4-quart saucepan, heat 5 inches of oil to 375F (190C) or until a 1-inch bread cube turns golden brown in about 50 seconds. If you have a tortilla basket fryer, use it to fry Tortilla Baskets, following manufacturer's directions. If not, you can create your own tortilla fryer from a 4-inch-diameter metal can with 1 end removed. Remove label from can; wash and dry can. Using tongs, hold can by top. Place 1 tortilla on surface of hot oil and quickly, carefully push tortilla into oil with can. Fry tortilla 1 to 2 minutes or until crisp and lightly browned, tipping can slightly so oil flows into center of tortilla. When tortilla is cooked, lift can with tortilla attached from oil. Drain carefully; set on paper towels to cool slightly. Protecting your hands, carefully twist can free. Drain on paper towels. Repeat with remaining tortillas. If preparing ahead, cool tortilla baskets. Cover loosely; store up to 3 days. Before filling, warm in a 350F (175C) oven, 5 minutes.

Tortilla Basket Salads for a Crowd; Guacamole, page 13; Eldora's Salsa, page 41.

How to Make Twice-as-Nice Lasagna Roll-Ups

1/Spread about 1-1/2 cups tomato sauce in each baking dish. Spread a thin layer of cheese filling evenly over each noodle.

2/Roll up filled lasagna noodles, jelly-roll style. Place seam-side down in baking dishes over tomato sauce.

Twice-as-Nice Lasagna Roll-Ups

A unique way of putting together two delicious meatless lasagnas — one for now and one for later.

2 (10-oz.) pkgs. frozen chopped spinach
3 (15-oz.) cans tomato sauce
1 (12-oz.) can tomato paste
1 medium onion, diced
1 tablespoon sugar
1 teaspoon dried leaf oregano, crushed
1 teaspoon dried leaf basil, crushed
1/2 teaspoon garlic salt

1 (16-oz.) pkg. lasagna noodles
32 oz. ricotta cheese or cottage cheese (4 cups)
4 cups shredded mozzarella cheese (1 lb.)
3 eggs, beaten
2 cups grated Parmesan cheese (6 oz.)
1 teaspoon salt
2 tablespoons dried parsley flakes
1/4 teaspoon ground nutmeg

Cook spinach according to package directions. Drain well, reserving cooking liquid. Set aside. In a large saucepan, combine reserved spinach cooking liquid, tomato sauce, tomato paste, onion, sugar, oregano, basil and garlic salt. Simmer, uncovered, 20 minutes over medium-low heat. Remove from heat; set aside. Cook lasagna noodles according to package directions. Drain; set aside. In a large bowl, combine drained spinach, ricotta cheese or cottage cheese, mozzarella cheese, eggs, 1 cup Parmesan cheese, salt, parsley flakes and nutmeg. Mix well. Set aside. Preheat oven to 350F (175C). Spread about 1-1/2 cups of the tomato sauce in each of 2 (9-inch-square) baking dishes. Lay 4 or 5 lasagna noodles flat on a working surface. Spread a thin layer of cheese filling evenly over each noodle. Roll up jelly-roll style; place, seam-side down, in baking dishes. Continue spreading and rolling remaining noodles. Pour remaining sauce evenly over rolled noodles in dishes. Sprinkle each dish with 1/2 cup Parmesan cheese. If preparing ahead, cover unbaked lasagna roll-ups tightly with foil and freeze up to 2 months. To serve, bake, uncovered, 45 minutes (50 to 60 minutes if frozen) or until heated through. Makes 2 casseroles, 6 to 8 servings each.

Make-Ahead Meat Loaf

When ground beef is on sale, buy five pounds and make it all into meat loaf. Serve one loaf right away; put the others in the freezer for future fuss-free meals.

5 lbs. lean ground beef
2 (8-oz.) cans tomato sauce
2 eggs
1/2 cup milk
1-1/2 teaspoons salt

1/2 teaspoon seasoned salt
1/2 teaspoon pepper
2 tablespoons instant minced onion
2 cups fine dry bread crumbs or
  cracker crumbs

Preheat oven to 350F (175C). Place beef in a very large bowl. In a small bowl, combine tomato sauce, eggs, milk, salt, seasoned salt, pepper and instant minced onion. Mix until blended; pour mixture over beef. Add bread crumbs; mix with your hands until ingredients are blended. Divide meat mixture in thirds. Put each portion into an 8'' x 4'' loaf pan. If preparing ahead, cover unbaked loaves tightly with foil; freeze up to 3 months. To serve, bake 1 hour (frozen, thawed loaves, 1-1/2 hours) or until meat in center is no longer pink. Makes 3 meat loaves, 6 to 8 servings each.

Variation

If you're preparing meat loaves to freeze, you may shape meat mixture into 3 (8'' x 4'') rectangles instead of placing in pans. Wrap each rectangle in heavy-duty foil; freeze up to 3 months. Put each rectangle in an 8'' x 4'' loaf pan before baking.

Double-Good Baked Broccoli

Use one casserole for dinner tonight; freeze the other for company later.

2 tablespoons butter or margarine
1 small onion, finely chopped
4 (10-oz.) pkgs. frozen broccoli spears,
  cooked, drained
2 (10-3/4-oz.) cans cream of mushroom soup

1 (10-3/4-oz.) can cream of chicken soup
1/2 cup slivered almonds
2 cups shredded Cheddar cheese (8 oz.)
1 cup fine dry bread crumbs

Preheat oven to 325F (165C). In a small skillet, melt butter or margarine; add onion and sauté until tender but not browned. Transfer onion to a medium bowl; stir in cooked broccoli. Butter 2 (1-1/2-quart) casserole dishes. Put 1/2 of broccoli mixture in each buttered dish. In a medium bowl, stir together soups, almonds and cheese; spoon evenly over broccoli mixture in each dish. Sprinkle casseroles evenly with bread crumbs. If preparing ahead, cover unbaked casseroles tightly with foil; freeze up to 2 months. To serve, bake, uncovered, 45 minutes to 1 hour (1 to 1-1/4 hours if frozen) or until heated through. Makes 2 casseroles, 6 to 8 servings each.

Variation

Substitute 3-1/2 pounds fresh broccoli, cut in spears, cooked, and drained, for the frozen broccoli.

Fresh Shell Cannelloni

We obtained this recipe from a cooking class taught by a good friend.

Cannelloni Filling, see below
1 (32-oz.) jar spaghetti sauce or
   1 qt. Spaghetti Sauce Supreme, page 45
4 eggs
1 cup all-purpose flour

1-1/4 cups water
1 teaspoon salt
About 2 tablespoons vegetable oil
4 cups shredded mozzarella cheese (1 lb.)

Cannelloni Filling:
32 oz. ricotta cheese (4 cups)
2 teaspoons dried leaf mint, crushed

3 eggs, beaten
3 tablespoons grated Parmesan cheese

Prepare Cannelloni Filling; set aside. Preheat oven to 350F (175C). Spread a spoonful of spaghetti sauce in each of 2 (9-inch-square) baking dishes. Set aside. In a medium bowl, beat eggs until light and frothy. Beat in flour. Gradually beat in water and salt. Lightly oil a 6- to 8-inch skillet with rounded sides; heat over medium-high heat. Pour about 2 tablespoons batter into skillet; tilt skillet quickly to evenly cover. Cook until dry around edge. Turn; lightly brown other side. Remove from skillet, place on paper towels and keep warm. Repeat with remaining batter, re-oiling skillet as needed. Place about 3 tablespoons of Cannelloni Filling on 1 side of each manicotti shell. Roll up shells into cylinders. Place rolled shells, seam-side down, in prepared baking dishes. Cover with remaining spaghetti sauce; top with cheese. If preparing ahead, cover cannelloni tightly with foil; refrigerate up to 24 hours or freeze up to 3 months. To serve, bake, uncovered, 20 to 30 minutes (30 to 40 minutes if frozen) or until heated through. Makes 2 casseroles, 6 servings each.

Cannelloni Filling:
In a large bowl, combine ricotta cheese, mint, eggs and Parmesan cheese.

Marzetti

This mildly seasoned Italian-style casserole appeals to children's delicate palates.

1 (12-oz.) pkg. egg noodles
2 tablespoons butter or margarine
2 large onions, chopped
2 cups sliced fresh mushrooms
2 lbs. lean ground beef
1 teaspoon salt
1/4 teaspoon pepper

1/2 teaspoon ground oregano
2 (10-3/4-oz.) cans tomato soup
1 (12-oz.) can tomato paste
2/3 cup water
2 tablespoons Worcestershire sauce
4 cups shredded Cheddar cheese (1 lb.)

Preheat oven to 375F (190C). Butter 2 (2-quart) casserole dishes. Cook noodles according to package directions. Drain; set aside. In a large skillet, melt 2 tablespoons butter or margarine. Add onions and mushrooms; sauté 5 to 6 minutes or until onions are tender. Crumble in beef; continue to cook, stirring, until meat has lost its pink color. Drain off fat. Add salt, pepper, oregano, tomato soup, tomato paste, water and Worcestershire sauce. Cover and simmer 15 minutes. Stir in drained noodles and 2 cups cheese. Divide mixture evenly between buttered dishes. Top each casserole with 1 cup cheese. If preparing ahead, cover unbaked casseroles tightly with foil and freeze up to 3 months. To serve, bake, uncovered, 45 to 55 minutes (1 to 1-1/4 hours if frozen) or until heated through. Makes 2 casseroles, 6 to 8 servings each.

Fresh Shell Cannelloni

Frozen Fruit Combo

Make this fresh-fruit treat when peaches and pears are in abundance — then enjoy it all year long.

Juice of 6 oranges (about 3 cups)
Juice of 4 lemons (about 3/4 cup)
2-1/2 cups sugar
12 large peaches, peeled, sliced

8 large pears, peeled, sliced
2 lbs. seedless green grapes
1 (20-oz.) can pineapple tidbits, drained

In a medium saucepan, combine orange juice, lemon juice and sugar. Bring to a boil, stirring until sugar is dissolved. Remove from heat; cool. In a large bowl, combine peaches, pears, grapes and pineapple. Pour juice mixture over fruit; stir until blended. Ladle into 8 (1-pint) jars or freezer containers, leaving 1/2 inch headspace. Attach lids; freeze up to 12 months. At serving time, thaw mixture slightly; spoon into shallow dessert bowls. Makes 8 pints, 3 or 4 servings per pint.

Sweet Chocolate Cream Pie

Any meal can have a sweet ending when you keep one of these pies on hand in your freezer.

3 (9-inch) Graham-Cracker Pie Crusts,
    see below
1/2 cup vegetable shortening
3/4 cup sifted unsweetened cocoa powder
1-1/4 cups sugar
1 (8-oz.) pkg. cream cheese,
    room temperature

1 cup milk
3 (8-oz.) cartons frozen whipped topping,
    thawed
Sweetened whipped cream
Shaved unsweetened or semisweet chocolate,
    if desired

Graham-Cracker Pie Crusts:
1 (16-oz.) pkg. graham crackers
1 cup butter or margarine, melted

Prepare Graham-Cracker Pie Crusts; set aside. In a medium saucepan, melt shortening. Stir in cocoa powder until smooth. Remove from heat; cool. In a large bowl, cream sugar and cream cheese. Add milk and cocoa mixture; beat until smooth. Fold in whipped topping. Spoon mixture evenly into prepared crusts. Cover; freeze until firm. If preparing ahead, wrap frozen pies in foil; freeze up to 3 months. Remove from freezer 30 to 40 minutes before serving. Garnish with whipped cream and shaved chocolate, if desired. Makes 3 pies, 6 to 8 servings each.

Graham-Cracker Pie Crusts:
Preheat oven to 375F (190C). In a blender or a food processor fitted with a metal blade, process graham crackers until finely crushed. Place crumbs in a large bowl. Stir in melted butter or margarine until blended. Place 1/3 of the crumb mixture in each of 3 (9-inch) pie plates; press to cover bottoms and sides of pie plates evenly. Bake 8 to 10 minutes. Cool. Makes 3 Graham-Cracker Pie Crusts.

Variations
You may substitute 3 (4-oz.) pkgs. sweet baking chocolate for the cocoa powder. Reduce sugar to 6 tablespoons. Melt chocolate with shortening, stirring constantly.

Big-Batch Freezer Pie Crust

Our favorite!

6 cups all-purpose flour
2 teaspoons salt
1 (1-lb.) can vegetable shortening
   (2-1/3 cups)

1-1/3 cups cold water

Cut 7 (12-inch) squares of plastic wrap or wax paper; also cut 7 (12-inch) squares of foil. Set aside. In a large bowl, stir together flour and salt. With a pastry blender or 2 knives, cut in shortening until mixture resembles cornmeal. Add cold water all at once. Mix lightly with a fork until water is absorbed and mixture forms a ball. Divide dough into 7 equal portions; then shape each portion into a ball. Flatten each ball slightly. Wrap each flattened ball in 1 piece of plastic wrap or wax paper. Place 1 wrapped ball on each piece of foil. Fold foil tightly against ball, making an airtight seal. Freeze up to 10 months. Makes 7 balls, each enough for 1 (9-inch) pastry shell.

To make 1 (9-inch) pastry shell:
Partially thaw 1 ball of Big-Batch Freezer Pie Crust. Roll out dough to a thin 11-inch circle between 2 sheets of lightly floured wax paper. Place dough, without stretching, in a 9-inch pie plate. Flute edge. If recipe calls for a baked pastry shell, preheat oven to 425F (220C). Bake pastry shell 10 to 12 minutes or until very lightly browned. Cool; fill and bake as recipe directs.

To make 1 (9-inch) double-crust pie:
Use 2 balls of Big-Batch Freezer Pie Crust. Roll out 1 ball; line pie plate as directed above. Fill pie. Roll out second ball; place top crust over filling. Seal and flute edge. Cut several slits in top crust to allow steam to escape.

Snickerdoodle Cookie Rolls

Here's a convenient slice-and-bake form of an old favorite.

2 cups vegetable shortening
3 cups sugar
4 eggs
5-1/3 cups all-purpose flour
4 teaspoons cream of tartar

2 teaspoons baking soda
1 teaspoon salt
1 teaspoon ground cinnamon
2 tablespoons sugar

Cut 4 (14'' x 12'') pieces of wax paper or plastic wrap; set aside. In a large bowl, cream shortening and 3 cups sugar until smooth. Beat in eggs until light and fluffy. In a medium bowl, combine flour, cream of tartar, baking soda and salt. Gradually add flour mixture to creamed mixture, stirring until blended. Divide dough into 4 equal portions. Shape each portion into an 8- to 10-inch roll; wrap each roll in 1 piece of wax paper or plastic wrap. Place wrapped rolls in a freezer container with a tight-fitting lid, or wrap each roll airtight in a 14'' x 12'' piece of heavy foil. Freeze up to 6 months. Makes 4 rolls of dough, each enough for about 36 cookies.

To bake 1 roll of dough: Preheat oven to 400F (205C). Lightly grease 2 large baking sheets. In a small bowl, combine 1 teaspoon ground cinnamon and 2 tablespoons sugar. Cut frozen dough in 1/4-inch-thick slices. Dip each slice in cinnamon-sugar mixture. Place coated slices, sugared-side up, 1 to 1-1/2 inches apart on greased baking sheets. Bake 10 minutes or until edges are browned and centers are set and slightly cracked. Cool 2 minutes on baking sheets. Remove from baking sheets; cool on racks. Makes about 36 cookies.

Twinkettes

These cupcakes require no frosting; they're filled with a sweet vanilla cream, just like the commercial brand.

1 (18-1/4-oz.) pkg. lemon-flavored
   cake mix, plus ingredients listed
   on package to make cake

1 (18-1/4-oz.) pkg. yellow-cake mix,
   plus ingredients listed on package
   to make cake

1 (18-1/4-oz.) pkg. pineapple-flavored
   cake mix, plus ingredients listed
   on package to make cake

French-Vanilla Filling, see below

French-Vanilla Filling:

5 tablespoons all-purpose flour

5 tablespoons sugar

1 cup milk

1/2 cup butter or margarine,
   room temperature

1/2 cup vegetable shortening

1 cup sugar

1 teaspoon vanilla extract

Dash of salt

Preheat oven to 350F (175C). Line about 80 muffin cups with paper baking cups, or grease muffin cups well. In a very large bowl, combine all 3 cake mixes. Add ingredients to make cakes according to package directions. Pour batter into prepared muffin cups; fill each cup 2/3 full. Bake, in batches, 15 minutes or until tops spring back when lightly touched. Turn out of pans; cool on racks. Prepare French-Vanilla Filling; spoon into a pastry bag fitted with a No. 9, 10 or 11 tip. Insert tip into center of each cooled cupcake. Squeeze bag to force filling into cupcake, rotating cupcake as you squeeze bag. Refrigerate filled cupcakes. If preparing ahead, place cupcakes in freezer containers, cover tightly and freeze up to 3 months. Makes about 80 cupcakes.

French-Vanilla Filling:

In a small saucepan, stir together flour and 5 tablespoons sugar. Add milk; stir until smooth. Cook over medium heat, stirring, until thick. Remove from heat; cool. In a medium bowl, cream butter or margarine, shortening, 1 cup sugar, vanilla and salt. Add cooled milk mixture; beat with an electric mixer 5 minutes or until fluffy.

Variation

If pineapple-flavored cake mix is not available, substitute white-cake mix, using unsweetened pineapple juice in place of the liquid called for on the package.

CHAPTER THREE

Plan-Overs

Plan to have leftovers when you buy, when you cook and when you eat. "Plan-over" cooking is the chef's way to avoid wasting food and time in the kitchen: you can watch your budget as well as the clock and experience a new kind of daylight savings time.

Plan-over meals can introduce variety into your menus and provide relief for your already strained pocketbook. But as the name suggests, this style of cooking does take planning. When you buy, take better advantage of sale items by purchasing more than enough for one meal. Buying extra won't take even a minute more at the market, and it saves you plenty of time later on—you'll have the makings for several bargain-price dinners on hand in your freezer.

When you cook, cook extra and have a plan in mind for using the leftovers. For example, if you're roasting a turkey, decide in advance how you want to serve it the next time around. Package leftover meat in meal-size portions and refrigerate or freeze for casseroles, salads and sandwiches. Store leftover gravy for use in stews and soups. Plan to use the *whole* turkey, right down to the carcass for Stretch-the-Turkey Soup. The secret here is to "take charge" of your leftovers. Incorporate them into your menu-planning; don't just let them accumulate in your refrigerator, then go to waste.

In this chapter, we show you how plan-over cooking works for roast beef, ham, pork, and turkey; you can apply the same concept to other foods as well. You'll find that turning one meal into more earns you triple dividends, saving time, money and energy.

> ### Beef, roast
> 1 lb. boneless = 2 cups diced or cubed; 2 cups shredded; 3 cups ground
> **Suggestions for use:** Use in beef Stroganoff, soups, sandwiches, hash.
> **Recipes included:** The Beef Connection, below; French Dip Sandwiches, page 58; Mini-Chimis, page 40; Saucy Beef Sandwiches, below; Stroganoff Beef Crepes, page 58; Basic Nine Recipes (Chapter 5), Crepes, page 109, Fried Rice, page 111, Make-a-Sandwich, page 122, Soups, page 114.

The Beef Connection

This recipe is well-named: it's sure to yield leftovers that will give you a "connection" to many entrees.

1 (7- to 9-lb.) beef top round roast	1/4 teaspoon dry mustard
1 (4-oz.) bottle browning and seasoning sauce	1/3 cup ketchup
2 garlic cloves, minced	6 drops hot-pepper sauce
1 tablespoon salt	1/2 teaspoon black pepper
1 teaspoon celery salt	2 teaspoons monosodium glutamate
2 medium onions, chopped	3 bay leaves
4 medium carrots, chopped	2 tablespoons dried parsley flakes
4 celery stalks, chopped	

Place roast in a large roasting pan. Cover with browning and seasoning sauce. Sprinkle garlic, salt, celery salt, onions, carrots and celery on roast. Make a short, 1/4-inch-deep slit in top of roast; insert mustard. Drizzle ketchup over top of roast. Sprinkle with hot-pepper sauce, black pepper, monosodium glutamate, bay leaves and parsley flakes. Half-fill pan with water. Cover with foil and bake in a 275F (135C) oven, 5-1/2 hours for medium, a meat thermometer inserted in thickest part of roast will register 160F (70C), or until done to your liking. Strain pan juices; discard vegetables and bay leaves. Let roast stand 10 minutes before carving. Serve sliced meat *au jus* (with meat juices). Makes 25 servings, about 1/3 pound meat per serving.

Saucy Beef Sandwiches

Capers give this creamy sauce a gourmet touch.

1/2 cup dairy sour cream	Lettuce Leaves
2 tablespoons white-wine vinegar	6 French rolls or thick slices
1-1/2 teaspoons prepared mustard	French bread
1-1/2 teaspoons sugar	12 slices roast beef
1/2 teaspoon salt	Red onion rings
1 teaspoon capers, drained	Cherry tomatoes

Stir together sour cream, vinegar, mustard, sugar and salt; blend well. Stir in capers; set aside. Place lettuce leaves atop French roll halves or bread slices. Top lettuce rolls with 2 slices beef. Drizzle with sauce. Top with onion rings. Garnish with cherry tomatoes. Makes 6 servings.

Saucy Beef Sandwiches

French Dip Sandwiches

Baked beans and a fruit salad are delicious accompaniments for this sandwich.

1-1/2 lbs. thinly sliced cooked top round roast from The Beef Connection, page 56
2 cups strained cooking juices from The Beef Connection, page 56

4 to 6 (4-inch-long) French rolls, split
Prepared mustard, if desired
Prepared horseradish, if desired

Place sliced beef and cooking juices in a medium saucepan. Heat thoroughly. Lift beef from juices. If desired, dip rolls in juices; then place a few slices of beef on each roll. Serve with additional cooking juices, mustard and horseradish, if desired. Makes 4 to 6 servings.

Tip
When serving French Dip Sandwiches, allow about 1/4 pound of meat and 1/3 cup of cooking juices per serving.

Stroganoff Beef Crepes

An out-of-the-ordinary encore for roast beef.

12 Basic Crepes, page 109
1/4 cup butter or margarine
1/4 lb. fresh mushrooms, sliced
1 small onion, chopped
1/3 cup cold water
3 tablespoons all-purpose flour
1/2 cup hot strained cooking juices from The Beef Connection, page 56, or hot beef broth

1 tablespoon ketchup
1 tablespoon Worcestershire sauce
1/2 teaspoon salt
1/8 teaspoon pepper
2 cups cubed roast beef (about 1 lb.) from The Beef Connection, page 56
3/4 cup dairy sour cream

Prepare crepes; keep warm. In a large skillet, melt butter or margarine. Add mushrooms and onion; sauté until onion is tender but not browned. In a small bowl, stir together cold water and flour. Stir in hot cooking juices or broth; pour into skillet. Stir in ketchup, Worcestershire sauce, salt and pepper. Cook over medium heat, stirring constantly, until mixture is thickened. Stir in beef; continue to cook until heated through. Blend in sour cream; cook until mixture is warm, but do not boil or sauce may curdle. Spoon about 1/4 cup of the beef mixture in center of each crepe; roll up. Spoon a small amount of beef mixture over crepes, if desired. Serve immediately. Makes about 6 servings.

Ham

1 lb. boneless = 2 cups diced or cubed; 3 cups ground

Suggestions for use: Use in scrambled eggs, sandwiches, casseroles; use with beans.

Recipes included: Basic Baked Ham, below; Ham Jambalaya, page 61; Ham Pithivier, page 62; Julie's Ham Loaves, page 60; Swiss Gougère with Ham & Mushrooms, page 61; Basic Nine recipes (Chapter 5): Crepes, page 109, Fried Rice, page 111, Make-a-Sandwich, page 123, Omelets, page 112, Quiches, page 119, Salads, page 116.

Basic Baked Ham

This recipe works well for boneless ham, too; just decrease the baking time.

4 to 7 lbs. bone-in fully cooked ham
1 (28-oz.) bottle ginger ale

Cherry Sauce, if desired, see below

Cherry Sauce:
1 (21-oz.) can cherry-pie filling
1 large orange

Place ham, fat-side up, on a rack in a shallow roasting pan. Pour ginger ale over ham; cover with foil. Bake in a 325F (165C) oven, 3 hours or until heated through. Prepare Cherry Sauce, if desired. Slice ham; serve with Cherry Sauce. Makes 8 to 14 servings, 1/4 to 1/3 pound meat per serving.

Cherry Sauce:
Place cherry-pie filling in a medium saucepan. Peel orange. Cut 1/2 of the peel, colored part only, into slivers; discard remaining peel. Juice orange. Stir juice and slivered peel into cherry-pie filling in saucepan. Cook until heated through. Makes 2-1/2 cups.

How to Make Julie's Ham Loaves

1/Flatten meat mixture in mixing bowl. Using rubber spatula, divide ham mixture into 12 equal portions. Shape each portion into a ball.

2/Top baked meat loaves with Sweet & Sour Mustard Sauce. Serve with Stir-Fry Vegetable Medley, page 22, and parsleyed rice.

Julie's Ham Loaves

The tantalizing sauce makes these individual ham loaves a real favorite.

1 lb. ground cooked ham (3 cups)
   from Basic Baked Ham, page 59
1 lb. ground pork
2 eggs, beaten
1 cup fine dry bread crumbs
3/4 cup milk

1 teaspoon dry mustard
2 tablespoons prepared horseradish
1 small onion, grated
1/4 teaspoon pepper
Sweet & Sour Mustard Sauce, see below

Sweet & Sour Mustard Sauce:
1-1/4 cups water
2 tablespoons cornstarch
1/2 cup packed brown sugar
1/4 cup white vinegar

2 teaspoons dry mustard
1/4 teaspoon salt
Dash of black pepper
Dash of red (cayenne) pepper

Lightly grease 12 (2-1/2-inch) muffin cups. In a large bowl, combine ham, pork, eggs, bread crumbs, milk, mustard, horseradish, onion and pepper. Divide into 12 equal portions; shape each into a ball. Place balls in greased muffin cups. Bake in a 350F (175C) oven, about 1 hour or until meat in center of loaves is no longer pink. Prepare Sweet & Sour Mustard Sauce; serve warm sauce over ham loaves. Makes 6 servings.

Sweet & Sour Mustard Sauce:

In a small saucepan, stir together water and cornstarch. Stir in brown sugar, vinegar, mustard, salt, black pepper and red pepper. Bring to a boil, stirring constantly; continue to boil until thickened. Makes about 1-3/4 cups.

Swiss Gougère with Ham & Mushrooms

Something different for supper: a Swiss-cheese-flavored cream-puff ring filled with creamed ham.

1/4 cup butter or margarine
1 small onion, finely chopped
1/4 lb. fresh mushrooms, sliced
1-1/2 tablespoons all-purpose flour
1/4 teaspoon pepper
1 cup milk
1-1/2 cups cooked ham, in 1-1/2- to
   2-inch-long strips, from Basic
   Baked Ham, page 59

Salt to taste
1 cup water
1/2 cup butter or margarine, cut in
   8 equal pieces
1 cup all-purpose flour
1/4 teaspoon salt
4 large eggs
1 cup finely shredded Swiss cheese (4 oz.)

In a medium skillet, melt 1/4 cup butter or margarine. Add onion; sauté until tender but not browned. Add mushrooms; sauté 2 more minutes. Stir in 1-1/2 tablespoons flour and pepper until blended. Cook, stirring, about 1 minute. Slowly add milk until smooth. Continue to cook, stirring, until bubbly and thickened. Remove from heat; stir in ham and salt to taste. Set aside. Preheat oven to 400F (205C). Butter a 10- to 12-inch ovenproof skillet or a 10- to 12-inch shallow baking dish. In a medium saucepan, combine water and 1/2 cup butter or margarine. Bring to a boil over medium-high heat. Add 1 cup flour and 1/4 teaspoon salt all at once. Stir vigorously about 1 minute or until mixture forms a ball in center of pan. Remove from heat; cool slightly. Add eggs, 1 at a time, beating well with a wooden spoon after each addition. Stir in cheese. Drop dough by large spoonfuls in a ring around edge of buttered skillet or dish, leaving center open. Pour ham filling into center. Bake 20 minutes. Reduce oven temperature to 350F (175C) and continue to bake 25 more minutes. Serve immediately. Makes 6 servings.

Ham Jambalaya

This dish improves in flavor if made ahead and reheated.

3 tablespoons butter or margarine
1 cup chopped onions
1 cup uncooked long-grain white rice
1 (29-oz.) can tomatoes
1/2 cup diced green bell pepper
1/2 teaspoon ground thyme
1/2 teaspoon dried leaf basil, crushed
1/2 teaspoon ground marjoram
1/2 teaspoon ground allspice
1 chicken bouillon cube
1 cup water

1 bay leaf
1/4 teaspoon black pepper
1/2 teaspoon paprika
1 tablespoon brown sugar
2 cups diced cooked ham (about 1 lb.) from
   Basic Baked Ham, page 59
2 tablespoons chopped fresh parsley,
   if desired
3/4 cup shredded Cheddar cheese (3 oz.),
   if desired

In a large saucepan, melt butter or margarine over medium heat. Add onions; sauté until tender-crisp. Add rice; stir until rice is barely golden. Cut tomatoes in quarters; add tomatoes and their juice to rice along with bell pepper, thyme, basil, marjoram, allspice, bouillon cube, water, bay leaf, black pepper, paprika and brown sugar. Stir in ham; bring mixture to a boil. Reduce heat. Cover; simmer 20 to 25 minutes or until rice is tender. Spoon into a large serving bowl. If desired, sprinkle parsley over center of jambalaya and cheese around edges. Makes 6 to 8 servings.

Ham Pithivier

A beautiful luncheon entree that tastes as good as it looks.

Egg Glaze, see below
2 egg yolks
1/4 cup whipping cream
1/4 teaspoon Worcestershire sauce
1 drop hot-pepper sauce
2 tablespoons butter or margarine
2 tablespoons thinly sliced green onion

1 cup finely chopped cooked ham from
  Basic Baked Ham, page 59
1/2 cup shredded Swiss cheese (2 oz.)
1 hard-cooked egg, chopped
Dash of black pepper
1 (10-oz.) pkg. frozen patty shells
  (6 patty shells), thawed

Egg Glaze:
1 egg, beaten
1/4 teaspoon salt

Prepare Egg Glaze; set aside. In a small bowl, combine egg yolks, cream, Worcestershire sauce and hot-pepper sauce. Set aside. In a medium skillet, melt butter or margarine over medium heat. Add green onion; sauté until soft. While stirring green onions, add egg-yolk mixture. Continue to cook, stirring, until mixture thickens; do not let mixture boil. Remove from heat; stir in ham, cheese, egg and black pepper. Refrigerate until cool. Between 2 sheets of lightly floured wax paper, arrange 3 thawed patty shells with edges slightly overlapping. Using a rolling pin, roll out to a circle about 8 inches in diameter. Using a round 8-inch baking pan as a guide, trim edges of pastry to make an 8-inch circle. Place pastry circle on an ungreased baking sheet. With fork tines, prick circle all over. Mound cooled ham mixture on pastry circle, leaving a 1-1/2-inch border. Lightly brush Egg Glaze around outside edge of circle, being careful not to let it drip over edge of pastry. Slightly overlap remaining 3 thawed patty shells between 2 sheets of lightly floured wax paper. Roll out to another 8-inch circle; trim edges as above. Position second circle over ham-topped pastry, stretching as necessary to match edges. Deflate any air pockets by pricking with a fork. Press edges firmly with your fingers to seal. Using the point of a knife, cut a 1/2-inch-diameter circle in center of top pastry. Also score top pastry with knife to make a design, making 1/16-inch-deep cuts; be careful not to cut all the way through pastry. Long, curved lines radiating from the center are the traditional design, but any pattern may be used. Brush top with Egg Glaze. Press all around edges of pastry with back of knife at 1/4-inch intervals to make a scallop design. Refrigerate at least 30 minutes or up to 24 hours. Preheat oven to 450F (230C). Bake 15 minutes. Reduce oven temperature to 400F (205C) and continue to bake 20 more minutes or until puffed and golden brown. If pastry begins to overbrown, cover it loosely with foil. Let stand 5 minutes before cutting. Cut in wedges to serve. Makes 4 to 6 servings.

Egg Glaze:
In a small bowl, beat together egg and salt.

How to Make Ham Pithivier

1/Between lightly floured wax paper, arrange 3 thawed patty shells with edges slightly overlapping. Roll out to an 8-inch circle; trim edges.

2/Mound cooled ham mixture on center of pastry circle. Roll out remaining 3 patty shells to an 8 inch circle. Position over ham mixture, stretching slightly to match pastry edges.

3/Press moistened edges to seal. Using point of a knife, cut a 1/2-inch-diameter circle in center of top pastry. Score top as shown. Press edge with back of a knife to make a scallop design.

4/Bake 15 minutes; reduce oven temperature and bake 20 minutes longer or until puffed and golden brown. To serve, cut in wedges.

Pork, roast

1 lb. boneless = 1-1/2 to 2 cups diced or cubed

Suggestions for use: Use in casseroles, fried rice, chow mein and Oriental noodle dishes; add to barbecue sauce and serve on sandwich rolls.

Recipes included: Chili Verde Sauce, opposite page; Basic Nine recipes (Chapter 5): Crepes, page 109, Fried Rice, page 111, Make-a-Sandwich, page 122, Pork-Roast Premier, below, Navajo Tacos With Chili Verde Sauce, page 66.

Pork-Roast Premier

This pork roast's encore appearance in Chili Verde Sauce, opposite, may win more applause than its first performance!

1 (5- to 6-lb.) bone-in pork loin roast
Salt and pepper to taste

Pork-Roast Gravy, see below

Pork-Roast Gravy:
Pan drippings from pork roast
All-purpose flour

Water
Salt and pepper to taste

Place roast on a rack in a roasting pan. Sprinkle with salt and pepper. Insert a meat thermometer in thickest part of roast (not touching bone). Bake in a 350F (175C) oven, 45 to 55 minutes per pound or until thermometer registers 165F (75C). Remove roast from oven; pour off drippings to use for Pork-Roast Gravy. Let roast stand 10 minutes before carving or until thermometer registers 170F (75C). Meanwhile, prepare gravy. Serve gravy with sliced meat. Save bones and any leftover meat and gravy to make Chili Verde Sauce, opposite page. Makes 8 to 10 servings, about 1/3 pound meat per serving.

Pork-Roast Gravy:

Measure pan drippings from pork roast. Remove excess fat. For every 1/2 cup of drippings, you will need 1/2 cup flour and about 4 cups water. To make gravy, place drippings in a medium saucepan over low heat. Stir in flour until blended; cook, stirring, about 1 minute or until bubbly. Slowly add water, stirring with a whisk until smooth. Continue to cook, stirring, until bubbly and thickened. Season with salt and pepper.

Chili Verde Sauce

A spicy, delicious meat-and-gravy topping for many of your favorite Mexican dishes.

Roast pork loin bones from
Pork-Roast Premier, opposite
1 to 2 cups cubed pork from
Pork-Roast Premier, opposite
8 cups water, chicken broth or
leftover pork gravy, or a combination
1/2 cup butter or margarine
1 large onion, chopped

3/4 cup all-purpose flour
1 tablespoon garlic salt
1 teaspoon ground oregano
1 teaspoon ground cumin
1 (4-oz.) can diced green chilies
1 (8-oz.) bottle red taco sauce or
1 (7-oz.) can green-chili salsa
1/2 cup water, if necessary

Place pork bones and cubed pork in a large Dutch oven. Add 8 cups water, broth, or gravy. Bring to a boil; reduce heat. Cover; simmer 3 to 4 hours or until all meat falls from bones. Remove from heat; let stand until cool enough to handle. Remove all bones from mixture; skim off fat. In a medium skillet, melt butter or margarine. Add onion; sauté until tender but not browned. Stir in flour until blended. Stir in garlic salt, oregano and cumin. Add a small amount of broth from meat mixture, stirring with a whisk. Then stir flour mixture into meat mixture in Dutch oven, blending until smooth. Add chilies and taco sauce or green-chili salsa. Heat until thickened, stirring frequently. Add 1/2 cup more water, if necessary, to thin to desired consistency. Makes about 1-1/2 quarts.

Variation
For a spicier sauce, add an additional (4-oz.) can of diced green chilies.

How to Make Navajo Tacos with Chili Verde Sauce

1/Roll out each piece of dough to a 6-inch circle. With fingers, poke a hole in center of each dough circle. Lower dough into hot oil, 1 at a time. Fry until golden brown; turn and brown other side.

2/Top each Fry Bread with beans, Chili Verde Sauce, cheese, lettuce, olives tomatoes, green onions, sour cream and avocado. Serve immediately.

Navajo Tacos with Chili Verde Sauce

Here's an ideal entree for a Mexican-style buffet supper.

Fry Bread, see below
1 (40-1/2-oz.) can refried beans
5 cups shredded Colby cheese (1-1/4 lbs.)
1 large head iceberg lettuce, shredded
2 large avocados, pitted, peeled, diced

2 large tomatoes, diced
1/2 to 3/4 cup chopped green onions
3/4 cup chopped black olives
3 cups Chili Verde Sauce, page 65, heated
1 pint dairy sour cream (2 cups)

Fry Bread:
4 cups all-purpose flour
1 tablespoon salt
1/3 cup vegetable shortening

1-1/2 cups warm water
Vegetable oil for deep-frying

Prepare Fry Bread; keep warm. In a medium saucepan, warm beans until heated through. Arrange cheese, lettuce, avocados, tomatoes, green onions and olives on a platter. To assemble each taco, place 1 piece of Fry Bread on a serving plate. Top with beans, Chili Verde Sauce, cheese, lettuce, avocados, tomatoes, green onions, olives and sour cream. Serve immediately. Makes 12 to 16 servings.
Fry Bread:
In a large bowl, stir together flour and salt. Using 2 knives or a pastry blender, cut in shortening until mixture resembles cornmeal. Add warm water to make a soft, but not sticky dough. Let dough rest 15 minutes. Divide dough into 16 equal portions; shape each into a ball. In a large skillet, heat 1/2 inch of oil to 375F (190C). Poke a hole in center of each circle of dough. Lower dough circles, 1 at a time, into hot oil. Fry until golden brown on 1 side. Turn over; fry until browned on other side. Drain on paper towels.

Turkey, roast

1 lb. boneless = 2 cups diced or cubed

Suggestions for use: Use in casseroles, salads, hot or cold sandwiches.

Recipes included: Basic Roast Turkey, below, Curried Turkey Bombay, page 70, Fruited Turkey Salad, page 70, Gourmet Turkey Sandwich, page 69, Stretch-the-Turkey Soup, page 72, Turkey Bonbons, page 68, Turkey-in-the-Rye, page 69, Turkey Quickies, page 72, Basic Nine recipes (Chapter 5): Crepes, page 109, Make-a-Sandwich, page 122, Quiches, page 119, Salads, page 116, Soups, page 114.

Turkey gravy

Suggestions for use: Use as topping for meat loaf, pot pies, hash, croquettes, crepes, rice, hot meat sandwiches; add to soups or stews.

Recipes included: Stretch-the-Turkey Soup, page 72; Turkey Bonbons, page 68; Basic Nine recipes (Chapter 5): Crepes, page 109, Make-a-Sandwich, page 122.

Basic Roast Turkey

You may roast the turkey with or without the basting sauce. Fines herbes is a combination of equal parts dried leaf thyme, oregano, marjoram, basil, rosemary and rubbed sage.

**Herbed Basting Sauce, if desired,
  see below**
Super Stuffing, if desired, page 129

1 turkey with giblets, thawed if frozen
Salt
Basic Turkey Gravy, if desired, page 68

Herbed Basting Sauce:
1/2 cup butter or margarine
2 teaspoons fines herbes

1/2 teaspoon onion salt
1/4 teaspoon celery salt, if desired

Prepare Herbed Basting Sauce, if desired. Set aside. Prepare stuffing, if desired. Preheat oven to 325F (165C). Remove giblets and neck from turkey; reserve to use in gravy, if desired. Rinse cavity of bird; pat dry with paper towels. Sprinkle lightly with salt. If using stuffing, loosely pack stuffing into body and neck cavities. Skewer neck cavity closed or place flap of extra skin over stuffing to keep it inside. Tie ends of legs together or tuck legs under wire clip, if present. Place bird, breast up, on a rack in a shallow roasting pan. Brush with Herbed Basting Sauce, if desired, using all the sauce. Roast for time specified on turkey wrapper. When bird is done, a thermometer inserted into thickest part of thigh (not touching bone) should register 185F (85C). If bird begins to get too brown during last part of roasting, cover it with a foil tent. Let turkey stand 15 minutes before carving. Meanwhile, prepare gravy from drippings, if desired. Serve gravy with sliced meat. Number of servings depends on size of turkey; plan on about 1 serving per pound.

Herbed Basting Sauce:

In a small saucepan, melt butter or margarine. Stir in fines herbes, onion salt and celery salt, if desired. Use to brush over turkey before roasting.

Basic Turkey Gravy

Your gravy is guaranteed lump-free if you shake water and flour together until smooth.

Pan drippings from Basic Roast Turkey,
   page 67
1 cup water
1/2 cup all-purpose flour
2 cups chicken broth or water

1/4 teaspoon ground thyme
1/4 teaspoon ground sage
1/4 teaspoon onion salt
Salt and pepper to taste

Measure pan drippings; remove excess fat, pour 1/2 cup drippings back into roasting pan. Reserve any additional drippings for other uses, if desired. In a 1-pint jar with a tight-fitting lid, combine 1 cup water and flour. Secure lid tightly; shake vigorously until smooth. Add flour mixture to drippings in pan; stir well with a whisk. Cook over medium heat, gradually adding 2 cups broth or water, thyme, sage, onion salt, salt and pepper. Cook, stirring constantly, until bubbly and thickened. Makes about 3-1/2 cups.

Variation
For giblet gravy, place neck and giblets, except liver, in a saucepan. Cover with water; bring to a boil. Reduce heat. Cover; simmer 1-1/2 hours or until gizzard is tender. Add liver during last 10 minutes of cooking, if desired. Remove giblets and neck from broth; chop meat finely. Chop liver, if used. Add chopped giblets, neck meat and liver, if used, to gravy.

Turkey Bonbons

Each savory bonbon holds a surprise: a center of tart-sweet cranberry sauce.

1/4 cup butter or margarine
1/2 cup finely diced celery
1/4 cup finely diced onion
2 cups finely chopped cooked turkey from
   Basic Roast Turkey, page 67
1 cup crushed saltine crackers
1/2 teaspoon ground sage
1/8 teaspoon ground marjoram
1/8 teaspoon ground nutmeg

1/8 teaspoon dried leaf thyme, crushed
1/2 teaspoon salt
1/4 teaspoon pepper
2 eggs, beaten
About 1/3 (16-oz.) can jellied cranberry
   sauce, cut into 3/4-inch cubes
2 cups Basic Turkey Gravy, above,
   if desired

Grease a baking sheet. In a small saucepan, melt butter or margarine. Add celery and onion; sauté until tender but not browned. Transfer to a large bowl; add turkey, crushed crackers, sage, marjoram, nutmeg, thyme, salt, pepper and eggs. Mix until mixture holds together and can be molded. Divide mixture into 6 portions; form each portion around 1/6 of the cranberry-sauce cubes, making 6 (2-1/2-inch-diameter) balls. Place on greased baking sheet. Bake in a 375F (190C) oven, 20 minutes or until lightly browned. Serve with heated gravy, if desired. Makes 4 to 6 servings.

Turkey-in-the-Rye

Excellent idea for a luncheon; serve with fresh fruits in season.

Turkey Sauce Supreme, see below
6 dill-rye-bread slices
1 small to medium head iceberg lettuce, shredded
6 Swiss-cheese slices

6 (1/4-inch thick) cooked turkey-breast slices from Basic Roast Turkey, page 67
12 bacon slices, crisp-cooked, drained
6 cherry tomatoes

Turkey Sauce Supreme:
1 cup mayonnaise-style salad dressing
1/4 cup ketchup

5 tablespoons pineapple juice
1 tablespoon sugar

Prepare Turkey Sauce Supreme; refrigerate. For each sandwich, place 1 bread slice on a plate. Top with a bed of shredded lettuce. Top lettuce with a slice of cheese and a slice of turkey. Pour about 1/4 cup Turkey Sauce Supreme over each sandwich. Crisscross 2 bacon slices atop dressing on each sandwich. Garnish each open-faced sandwich with a cherry tomato. Pass additional Turkey Sauce Supreme, if desired. Makes 6 servings.

Turkey Sauce Supreme:
In a small bowl, combine salad dressing, ketchup, pineapple juice and sugar. Cover; refrigerate until needed. Makes about 1-1/2 cups.

Gourmet Turkey Sandwich

If you don't have leftover turkey breast, purchase a turkey breast from the delicatessen.

3 tablespoons butter or margarine
3 tablespoons all-purpose flour
1/2 teaspoon dry mustard
1/2 teaspoon salt
2 cups milk
1-1/3 cups shredded Longhorn cheese (5-1/3 oz.)

Pepper to taste
6 (1/2-inch thick) Italian- or French-bread slices
6 (1/4-inch thick) cooked turkey-breast slices from Basic Roast Turkey, page 67
1 (10-oz.) pkg. frozen broccoli spears, cooked, drained
1/2 teaspoon paprika

Preheat oven broiler. In a small saucepan, melt butter or margarine over medium heat. Stir in flour, mustard and salt until blended. Cook, stirring, for 1 minute or until bubbly. Gradually add milk, stirring with a whisk until smooth. Continue to cook, stirring constantly, until thickened. Stir in cheese until melted and smooth. Remove from heat. Season with pepper and set aside. Place bread in a single 13'' x 9'' baking dish. Toast, under broiler, lightly on both sides. Layer turkey and cooked broccoli on each toast slice. Pour cheese sauce over center part of each sandwich. Sprinkle with paprika. Broil 6 inches below heat source 5 minutes or until sauce begins to brown lightly. Serve hot. Makes 6 servings.

Fruited Turkey Salad

For a summer salad, serve in cantaloupe halves.

Sweet-Tart Dressing, see below
2 cups diced cooked turkey from
  Basic Roast Turkey, page 67
1 cup diagonally sliced celery
2 medium apples, cored, chopped
1 (20-oz.) can pineapple chunks, drained
1 cup seedless green grapes,
  cut in half horizontally

1/2 cup chopped walnuts, or
  sliced toasted almonds
1 banana, if desired, sliced
3 cantaloupes, halved and seeded
Lettuce leaves

Sweet-Tart Dressing:
3/4 cup dairy sour cream
3/4 cup mayonnaise

3 tablespoons honey
2 tablespoons fresh lemon or lime juice

Prepare Sweet-Tart Dressing; refrigerate. In a large bowl, combine turkey, celery, apples, pineapple, grapes, walnuts and banana, if desired. Toss with dressing, cover and refrigerate at least 1 hour. Serve in cantaloupe halves on lettuce-lined plates. Makes 6 servings.

Sweet-Tart Dressing:
In a small bowl, combine sour cream, mayonnaise, honey and lemon juice or lime juice. Cover; refrigerate. Makes about 1-1/2 cups.

Curried Turkey Bombay

The condiments make this an extra-special way to use leftover turkey.

1-1/2 cups uncooked long-grain white rice
1/4 cup butter or margarine
1 large onion, sliced
2 green apples, cored, sliced
3 tablespoons curry powder
1-1/2 cups turkey broth or chicken broth
1/2 cup apple juice
2 tablespoons ketchup

1/2 cup whipping cream
3 cups cubed cooked turkey from
  Basic Roast Turkey, page 67
Salt and pepper to taste
Condiments: Chutney, cashews or peanuts,
  mandarin oranges, flaked coconut and
  avocado slices, as desired

Cook rice according to package directions; keep warm. In a large skillet, melt butter or margarine. Add onion and apples; sauté 5 to 10 minutes or until apples are tender-crisp. Add curry powder; stir to coat. Add broth, apple juice and ketchup, stirring to combine all ingredients. Slowly stir in cream, then stir in turkey. Cook about 5 minutes or until turkey is heated through and sauce is slightly thickened. Season with salt and pepper. Serve over rice; pass condiments to top each serving. Makes 4 to 6 servings.

Fruited Turkey Salad

Stretch-the-Turkey Soup

You get the full value from your holiday bird when you make this delicious soup.

10 cups Turkey Stock, see below
1-1/2 cups chopped celery
1 cup chopped onions
2 cups sliced carrots
2 tablespoons chopped fresh parsley
1/4 teaspoon ground thyme

1 teaspoon salt
1/4 teaspoon pepper
2 cups uncooked egg noodles
1 cup frozen green peas
About 1/3 cup all-purpose flour
1 qt. milk (4 cups)

Turkey Stock:
Turkey carcass from Basic Roast Turkey,
**   page 67**
About 13 cups water

2 celery stalks
2 carrots, trimmed
1 onion, cut in quarters

Prepare Turkey Stock. In a large soup pot, combine Turkey Stock, celery, onions, carrots, parsley, thyme, salt and pepper. Bring to a boil over high heat. Reduce heat. Cover; simmer until vegetables are tender-crisp. Add noodles and peas; continue to cook until noodles are tender. Add any bits of meat left from making Turkey Stock. In a 1-pint jar with a tight-fitting lid, combine flour and 1 cup milk. Secure lid tightly. Shake vigorously until smooth. Gradually stir flour-mixture into soup. Stir in remaining 3 cups milk. Cook over medium heat, stirring, until soup is slightly thickened. Do not boil. Makes 6 to 8 servings.

Turkey Stock:
In a large soup pot or kettle, place entire turkey carcass, including any bits of meat that are still attached. Add about 13 cups water or enough to cover carcass completely. Add celery, carrots and onion. Cover; bring to a boil. Reduce heat; simmer 3 to 4 hours or until all meat falls from bones. Remove from heat. Strain broth; discard vegetables and bones. Reserve any pieces of meat to add to soup. Skim and discard fat from broth. Makes about 10 cups.

Turkey Quickies

Quick and easy tips for using your Thanksgiving turkey leftovers.

Speedy Turkey Casserole:
Butter a casserole dish. Place leftover dressing in bottom of buttered casserole dish. Layer sliced turkey and mashed potatoes over dressing; top with gravy. Cover and bake in a 325F (165C) oven, 25 minutes or until heated through.

Hot Turkey Sandwiches:
Place sliced leftover turkey in a saucepan. Add gravy; heat until bubbly. Toast slices of bread. Pour hot turkey and gravy over toast. Garnish each serving with a parsley sprig and a spiced crabapple.

Turkey Fruit Salad:
Toss cubed turkey with fresh pineapple cubes, red or green grapes, papaya chunks and avocado chunks. Spoon each serving onto a pineapple slice on a lettuce leaf. Garnish with your favorite creamy dressing and a maraschino cherry.

Baked Stuffing Balls:
Preheat oven to 375F (190C). Grease a baking sheet. Form moist leftover dressing into balls about 2 inches in diameter. Bake on greased baking sheets, in 375F (190C) oven, about 20 minutes. Heat any leftover gravy; spoon over stuffing balls.

Chicken, cooked

1 lb. boneless = 2 cups cooked diced or cubed

Suggestions for use: Use in casseroles, pot pies, salads, sandwich spreads, soups. Or use in place of turkey.

Recipes included: Gayle's Chicken Salad, below; Poulet D'Artichoke, below; Basic Nine recipes (Chapter 5): Crepes, page 109, Omelets, page 112, Fried Rice, page 111, Soups, page 114, Salads, page 116, Make-a-Sandwich, page 122.

Poulet D'Artichoke

You can use rinsed marinated artichoke hearts in place of water-packed artichoke hearts.

3 cups cubed cooked chicken
2 (14-oz.) cans artichoke hearts in water, rinsed, drained
2 (10-3/4-oz.) cans cream of chicken soup
1 cup mayonnaise

1 tablespoon lemon juice
1 teaspoon curry powder
2 cups shredded Cheddar cheese (8 oz.)
2 cups seasoned bread cubes or purchased seasoned croutons

Butter a 13'' x 9'' baking pan. Arrange chicken in buttered pan. Cut artichoke hearts in half; place on top of chicken. In a medium bowl, combine soup, mayonnaise, lemon juice and curry powder. Spread soup mixture over artichoke hearts. Sprinkle cheese on top; arrange bread cubes or croutons over all. Cover. If preparing ahead, refrigerate up to 24 hours. Bake, covered, in a 350F (175C) oven, 20 to 30 minutes. Continue to bake 5 to 10 more minutes or until heated through. Makes 6 servings.

Gayle's Chicken Salad

For an especially attractive presentation, serve this salad in scooped-out pineapple shells.

2 whole chicken breasts, cooked, diced
2 cups chopped celery
3 medium sweet pickles, diced
1 (4-oz.) can sliced black olives, drained
3 green onions, chopped
1 (15-1/4-oz.) can pineapple tidbits, drained
1 (2-oz.) pkg. sliced almonds, toasted
3 hard-cooked eggs, finely chopped

1 cup seedless green grapes, if desired
1 (8-oz.) can water chestnuts, if desired, drained, sliced
1-1/4 cups mayonnaise
2 teaspoons sugar
Salt and pepper to taste
Lettuce leaves

In a large bowl, combine chicken, celery, pickles, olives, green onions, pineapple, toasted almonds and eggs. Stir in grapes and water chestnuts, if desired; set aside. In a small bowl, stir together mayonnaise and sugar. Stir into chicken mixture; add salt and pepper. Cover; refrigerate several hours or up to 24 hours. Serve on lettuce leaves. Makes 6 to 8 servings.

Variation
Serve salad in pineapple shells. For every 4 shells, cut a whole pineapple in 4 wedges, leaving green tops attached. Scoop flesh out of each wedge leaving a 1/4 inch shell; substitute diced fresh pineapple for tidbits.

CHAPTER FOUR

Prepare Now, Serve Later

This "Prepare Now, Serve Later" section features dozens of recipes for dishes you can prepare at your convenience, then refrigerate or freeze to serve hours, days, weeks or even months later. If you're employed out of the home, you're sure to find this style of cooking appealing. With a made-ahead meal on hand, you needn't worry about rushing to the kitchen as soon as you arrive home in the evening. And if you like to entertain, you'll often choose recipes from this chapter. By doing almost all the cooking well in advance, you'll be free on the day of the party to clean house, set a beautiful table and enjoy your guests.

Both Marinated London Broil and Best-Ever Barbecued Spareribs are great neighborhood get-together fare. Either can be assembled 24 hours ahead, then put on the grill as the guests arrive. When you're expecting weekend company, make a truly elegant dessert and store it in the refrigerator or freezer until serving time. You'll find many recipes on these pages that are especially adaptable to open houses or buffets. Some of our top choices include Shrimp Mousse, Yummy Tuna-Cheese Balls, and Cocktail Franks. The foil dinners in this chapter can be a boon to the dieter in your group. It's difficult to prepare two separate meals, one for the weight-watchers and another for those who aren't counting calories.

Many of us experience days when we're simply too busy to cook. Plan-ahead for those days by making a main dish *now*. Later on, you can just pull it from refrigerator or freezer and slip it into the oven. We think you'll find this cooking method a great asset to your busy lifestyle.

Wassail

This winter-holiday drink will warm your guests and make your home smell terrific.

1-1/4 cups sugar
4 cups water
4 whole allspice
12 whole cloves
3 (2- to 3-inch) cinnamon sticks

1 (6-oz.) can frozen orange juice
    concentrate, reconstituted
1 (6-oz.) can frozen lemonade
    concentrate, reconstituted
8 cups apple cider

In a large kettle, combine sugar and water. Bring to a boil; boil 10 minutes. Reduce heat. On a 6-inch square of cheesecloth, place allspice, cloves and cinnamon sticks. Bring cloth up around spices; tie with a piece of thread. Add to kettle; simmer 1 hour. Add orange juice, lemonade and apple cider. Return to a boil; remove from heat. Cover; refrigerate until cool. Or pour into a large pitcher or jug; refrigerate up to 1 week. Heat wassail at serving time; remove spice bag just before serving. Makes about 4-1/2 quarts, 15 to 20 servings.

Eggnog-Punch Base

A nonalcoholic holiday favorite!

1/4 cup sugar
1/4 teaspoon ground cinnamon
1/4 teaspoon ground ginger
1/4 teaspoon ground cloves

6 eggs, beaten
8 cups orange juice
1/4 cup lemon juice

In a 3-quart pitcher with a lid, combine sugar, cinnamon, ginger, cloves, eggs, orange juice and lemon juice. Stir until sugar is dissolved. Cover; refrigerate until ready to make punch or up to 1 week. Makes about 2-1/2 quarts, enough base for 20 servings.

To make Eggnog Punch:
2-1/2 qts. Eggnog-Punch Base
1/2 gal. vanilla ice cream, slightly softened

2 (28-oz.) bottles ginger ale, chilled

Place Eggnog-Punch Base in a punch bowl. Add ice cream; stir gently until ice cream begins to melt. Add ginger ale. Serve immediately. Makes about 20 servings.

Piña Colada Drink Mix

This frosty drink helps cool you off on a hot summer day. And take note — it's made without alcohol.

4 cups pineapple juice
1 qt. milk (4 cups)

1-1/2 teaspoons coconut extract
2/3 cup sugar

Into a large pitcher, pour 2 cups pineapple juice, 2 cups milk, 3/4 teaspoon coconut extract and 1/3 cup sugar. Stir well. Pour into ice-cube trays; freeze. In the same pitcher, combine remaining 2 cups pineapple juice, 2 cups milk, 3/4 teaspoon coconut extract and sugar. Stir well. Cover; refrigerate up to 2 weeks. Makes 28 frozen cubes and about 1 quart refrigerated drink mix, enough base for 8 servings.

To make Piña Colada Drink:
7 frozen Piña Colada Drink Mix cubes
1 cup refrigerated Piña Colada Drink Mix

2 pineapple wedges
2 maraschino cherries with stems

In a blender, combine frozen Piña Colada Drink Mix cubes and refrigerated Piña Colada Drink Mix. Process until slushy. Pour into 2 glasses; garnish each serving with a pineapple wedge and a cherry. Makes 2 servings.

Shrimp Mousse   Photo on page 78.

The most requested recipe on our neighborhood holiday buffet table.

3 (4-1/2-oz.) cans small shrimp,
  rinsed, drained
1 (1/4-oz.) envelope unflavored gelatin
  (1 tablespoon)
1/4 cup cold water
1 (10-3/4-oz.) can tomato soup
1 (8-oz.) pkg. cream cheese,
  room temperature, cut in chunks

1 cup mayonnaise
3/4 cup finely chopped celery
1/2 cup finely chopped green onions
2 teaspoons lemon juice
Lemon slice
Fresh parsley sprigs
Crackers

Spray a 1- to 1-1/2-quart mold with vegetable cooking spray. Crumble drained shrimp into a bowl; set aside. In a small bowl, soften gelatin in cold water; set aside. In a small saucepan, warm soup over medium heat, stirring until smooth. Stir in softened gelatin. Add cream cheese; beat with an electric mixer on low speed until well blended. Stir in mayonnaise. Add shrimp, celery and green onions; stir to blend. Stir in lemon juice; pour into prepared mold. Refrigerate at least 4 hours or up to 24 hours. To unmold, moisten a chilled serving plate with a damp paper towel or pastry brush. With the tip of a sharp knife, carefully loosen mousse from edge of mold. Invert mold onto a serving plate. Wet a dishtowel in hot water; wring dry. Place hot, wet towel around mold. Leave on about 30 seconds. Remove mold and cloth. Garnish with parsley and a lemon slice bent into a "twist." Serve with crackers. Makes about 12 servings.

Shrimp Cocktail Sipper

Serve as an appetizer drink to accompany a cheese ball and crackers.

1 (48-oz.) can tomato juice
1 (7-oz.) can broken shrimp,
  rinsed, drained
3 or 4 drops hot-pepper sauce

1 teaspoon prepared horseradish
1/4 teaspoon onion salt
1/8 teaspoon garlic powder
Dash of black pepper

In a 2-quart container with a tight-fitting lid, combine all ingredients. Cover; refrigerate at least 8 hours or up to 24 hours. Makes 8 to 10 servings.

Hot Crab Dip

If you'd like to cut the cost of this delicious appetizer, substitute about 1 cup imitation crabmeat (now available in many supermarkets) for the canned crab.

1 (7-oz.) can crabmeat, drained
1 (8-oz.) pkg. cream cheese,
  room temperature
1/4 teaspoon salt

2 tablespoons chopped green onion
1 tablespoon milk
1 teaspoon prepared horseradish
1 (2-oz.) pkg. slivered almonds

In an ovenproof bowl, combine crabmeat, cream cheese, salt, green onion, milk and horseradish. Sprinkle almonds on top. If preparing ahead, cover unbaked mixture; refrigerate up to 24 hours. To serve, bake, uncovered, in a 350F (175C) oven, 20 minutes (about 30 minutes if refrigerated) or until heated through. Makes 10 to 12 servings.

Yummy Tuna-Cheese Balls   *Photo on page 78.*

Keep a few of these on hand in your freezer for impromptu entertaining.

4 (8-oz.) pkgs. cream cheese,
  room temperature
2 (6-1/4-oz.) cans solid-pack white
  tuna packed in water, drained
1 tablespoon lemon juice
3 celery stalks, finely chopped

3 tablespoons finely chopped green onions
1 green bell pepper, finely diced
1/2 teaspoon salt
1/8 teaspoon black pepper
1 cup finely chopped pecans or almonds
Crackers

In a large bowl, combine cream cheese, tuna, lemon juice, celery, green onions, bell pepper, salt and black pepper. Beat with an electric mixer until ingredients are evenly blended. Cut 5 (12-inch) squares of plastic wrap; set aside. Spread nuts on a plate. Divide cheese mixture into 5 portions; shape each portion into a ball. Roll each ball in nuts; wrap each in 1 square of plastic wrap. Refrigerate up to 3 days. Or wrap airtight in freezer wrap; freeze up to 8 months. Serve at room temperature with crackers. Makes 5 cheese balls.

Cocktail Franks

Keep a supply of fancy wooden picks and a spoon nearby to aid your guests in serving themselves.

2 tablespoons butter or margarine
1/3 cup chopped onion
1/4 cup chopped green bell pepper
1 (10-3/4-oz.) can tomato soup
2 tablespoons packed brown sugar

4 teaspoons Worcestershire sauce
1 tablespoon prepared mustard
1 tablespoon rice vinegar or
 white-wine vinegar
1 lb. cocktail franks

In a medium saucepan, melt butter or margarine. Add onion and bell pepper; sauté until onion is tender but not browned. Stir in soup, brown sugar, Worcestershire sauce, mustard and vinegar. Bring to a boil, stirring occasionally. Reduce heat; simmer, uncovered, 15 minutes. If preparing ahead, cool sauce. Pour into a container with a tight-fitting lid. Cover; refrigerate up to 1 week. To serve, combine sauce and cocktail franks in a medium saucepan; heat over medium-high heat until franks are thoroughly warmed. Serve in a chafing dish. If sauce is refrigerated, heat and serve as directed above. Makes 10 to 12 servings.

24-Hour Bean Dip

Serve this dip either cold or heated, with corn tortilla chips.

1 (17-oz.) can spicy refried beans
1-1/2 cups shredded Cheddar cheese (6 oz.)
1 (7-oz.) can green-chili salsa
1/2 green bell pepper, finely diced
1 (4-oz.) can chopped black olives, drained
1 small tomato, chopped

2 green onions, chopped
1 avocado, pitted, peeled, diced, tossed
 with lemon juice to prevent darkening
1/2 pint dairy sour cream (1 cup)
Fresh parsley sprig

Spread beans on a rimmed 12-inch platter. Sprinkle cheese over top. Spread salsa over cheese. Arrange bell pepper, olives, tomato, green onions, avocado and sour cream in concentric rings on top of salsa, working from outside towards center. Cover with plastic wrap; refrigerate at least 2 hours or up to 24 hours. To serve, garnish with a parsley sprig in center. Makes about 8 servings.

Variation
In an 11'' x 7'' baking dish, spread beans in an even layer; top with cheese. Preheat oven to 350F (175C). Bake, uncovered, until cheese is melted. Top with remaining ingredients as directed above.

Cocktail Franks; Wassail, page 75; Yummy Tuna-Cheese Ball, page 77; Shrimp Mousse, page 76; Dill Dip with fresh vegetables, page 37.

Country Cheese Soup

This recipe comes from one of our favorite restaurants.

2 large carrots, peeled, diced
1 onion, chopped
2 celery stalks, diced
8 cups water
2 tablespoons instant chicken-flavored
   bouillon

3/4 cup butter or margarine
3/4 cup all-purpose flour
1 (8-oz.) jar pasteurized process
   cheese spread
1 cup fresh or frozen green peas
1/4 teaspoon pepper

In a large kettle or Dutch oven, combine carrots, onion, celery, water and bouillon. Bring to a boil; reduce heat. Cover; simmer 10 minutes or until vegetables are tender. Meanwhile, in a small saucepan, melt butter or margarine. Add flour; stir until blended. Cook over low heat 2 to 3 minutes. Add to vegetable mixture, stirring with a whisk until thickened. Add cheese spread; stir until mixture is bubbly and thickened and cheese is melted. Add peas; simmer 10 minutes, stirring often. Serve hot. If preparing ahead, cool soup, cover, and refrigerate up to 24 hours. Reheat to serve. Makes 6 servings.

Our Favorite Gazpacho

Refreshing, nutritious and delightful. Be sure to prepare it at least 12 hours before serving.

4 cups tomato-clam juice
1/2 cup minced onion
1/3 cup vegetable oil
1/3 cup red-wine or white-wine vinegar
1/4 cup minced green bell pepper
3 tablespoons chopped fresh parsley
2 garlic cloves, minced
1/4 teaspoon hot-pepper sauce

1/4 teaspoon salt
Dash of black pepper
8 tomatoes, chopped
2 cucumbers, peeled, chopped
2 avocados, pitted, peeled, cubed
Garlic croutons
Grated Parmesan cheese

In a large bowl, combine tomato-clam juice, onion, oil, vinegar, bell pepper, parsley, garlic, hot-pepper sauce, salt and black pepper. Cover; refrigerate at least 6 hours or up to 2 days. Six hours before serving, add tomatoes, cucumbers and avocados. Serve very cold. Pass croutons and cheese to top each serving. Makes about 8 servings.

Tomatoes Vinaigrette

Try this as an accompaniment for grilled steaks.

3 medium tomatoes, cut in thick slices
1/2 cup olive oil
3 tablespoons red-wine or white-wine vinegar
1 teaspoon dried leaf oregano, crushed
1/2 teaspoon salt
1/4 teaspoon pepper

1/4 teaspoon dry mustard
1 garlic clove, minced
2 green onions, minced
1 tablespoon minced fresh parsley
Lettuce leaves

Arrange tomatoes in a shallow 11'' x 7'' dish, overlapping slices; set aside. In a small bowl, combine oil, vinegar, oregano, salt, pepper, mustard, garlic, green onions and parsley. Pour mixture over tomatoes. Cover; refrigerate at least 3 hours or up to 24 hours. Serve on lettuce leaves. Makes about 6 servings.

Potato Salad for a Crowd

The best potatoes for making potato salad are White Rose or red thin-skinned new potatoes.

5 lbs. potatoes, cooked, peeled,
    cubed (10 to 11 cups)
1/2 cup chopped green onions
1-1/2 cups thinly sliced celery
6 hard-cooked eggs, coarsely chopped
3/4 cup chopped sweet pickles

2 tablespoons sweet-pickle juice
2 teaspoons salt
1/4 teaspoon pepper
About 2 cups (1 recipe) Foundation
    Salad Dressing, page 118

In a very large bowl, combine potatoes, green onions, celery, eggs, pickles, pickle juice, salt and pepper. Toss lightly to distribute. Stir in Foundation Salad Dressing, cover and refrigerate at least 4 hours or up to 24 hours. Makes 12 to 15 servings.

Carrot-Orange Salad Supreme

One of our favorite ways to slip those carrots into our families' diets.

1 (6-oz.) pkg. orange-flavored gelatin
2 cups boiling water
1 cup orange juice
1 teaspoon grated orange peel

1 (15-1/4-oz.) can crushed pineapple
1 cup miniature marshmallows
1 cup finely grated carrots
1/2 pint whipping cream (1 cup), whipped

In a medium bowl, combine gelatin and boiling water. Stir until gelatin is dissolved. Stir in orange juice and orange peel. Refrigerate until slightly thickened. Fold in undrained pineapple, marshmallows and carrots. Fold in whipped cream. Pour into a 13'' x 9'' dish. Cover; refrigerate at least 2 hours or until firm, or up to 24 hours. Cut in squares to serve. Makes 12 to 16 servings.

Mandarin Salad in a Bag

Great tossed salad to prepare ahead and take with you to a potluck dinner or on a camping trip.

Dressing, see below
1 (2-oz.) pkg. sliced almonds
3 tablespoons sugar
1/2 head iceberg lettuce
1/2 head romaine lettuce

1 cup chopped celery
2 tablespoons chopped green onion
1 (11-oz.) can mandarin-orange sections,
  drained

Dressing:
1/4 cup vegetable oil
2 tablespoons white-wine vinegar
2 tablespoons sugar
1 tablespoon chopped fresh parsley

1/2 teaspoon salt
Dash of black pepper
Dash of hot-pepper sauce

Prepare Dressing; refrigerate. In a small skillet, combine almonds and sugar. Cook over low heat, stirring constantly, until almonds are coated and sugar is dissolved. Set aside to cool. Tear lettuces into bite-size pieces; place in a large plastic bag. Add celery and green onion. Close bag tightly; refrigerate up to 24 hours. To serve, pour Dressing and mandarin oranges into bag. Close bag tightly; shake until Dressing is evenly distributed. Add almonds; gently shake again. Makes 6 to 8 servings.
Dressing:
In a 1-pint jar with a tight-fitting lid, combine all dressing ingredients. Secure lid tightly; shake vigorously until ingredients are blended. Refrigerate until serving time. Shake again just before adding to salad.

Strawberry-Cream Squares

This recipe is perfect for serving at a ladies' luncheon.

1 (6-oz.) pkg. strawberry-flavored gelatin
2 cups boiling water
1 (10-oz.) pkg. frozen sweetened
  strawberries, partially thawed

1 (8-oz.) can crushed pineapple
2 bananas, diced
1/2 pint dairy sour cream (1 cup),
  room temperature

In a large bowl, combine gelatin and boiling water; stir until gelatin is dissolved. Break frozen strawberries apart; add to gelatin mixture, stirring until thawed. Add undrained crushed pineapple and bananas. Pour 1/2 of mixture into an 8-inch-square dish. Refrigerate until softly set. Spread sour cream over gelatin layer; carefully pour remaining gelatin mixture over top of sour cream. Cover; refrigerate at least 2 hours or until firm, or up to 24 hours. Cut in squares to serve. Makes 9 to 12 servings.

How to Make Holiday-Ribbon Salad

1/Prepare and set lime-flavored gelatin. Prepare cream-cheese mixture; pour over set gelatin. Smooth top with spoon. Refrigerate about 1 hour or until set.

2/Top with partially set strawberry-flavored gelatin. Cover; refrigerate until firm. To serve, cut in squares.

Holiday-Ribbon Salad

Delicious for any holiday dinner or buffet—just change the color of the gelatin to suit the occasion.

1 (6-oz.) pkg. lime-flavored gelatin
1-1/2 cups boiling water
1-1/2 cups cold water
1 (8-oz.) can crushed pineapple
Boiling water
1 (3-oz.) pkg. lemon-flavored gelatin

2 cups miniature marshmallows
1 (8-oz.) pkg. cream cheese, room temperature
1/2 pint whipping cream (1 cup), whipped
1 (6-oz.) pkg. strawberry-flavored gelatin
1-1/2 cups boiling water
1-1/2 cups cold water

In a medium bowl, combine lime-flavored gelatin and 1-1/2 cups boiling water. Stir until gelatin is dissolved. Stir in 1-1/2 cups cold water. Pour into a 13'' x 9'' dish. Refrigerate until almost firm. Drain juice from pineapple; add enough boiling water to make 1-1/2 cups liquid. Pour into a medium bowl; add lemon-flavored gelatin and marshmallows. Stir until marshmallows are melted. Cool slightly. In a medium bowl, beat cream cheese until smooth. Stir in drained pineapple and cooled lemon-gelatin mixture. Fold in whipped cream. Pour over set gelatin layer in dish. Refrigerate about 1 hour. In a medium bowl, combine strawberry-flavored gelatin and 1-1/2 cups boiling water. Stir in remaining 1-1/2 cups cold water. Cover; refrigerate until thickened and very syrupy. Carefully pour over set lemon mixture. Cover; refrigerate at least 2 hours or until firm, or up to 24 hours. Cut in squares to serve. Makes 15 to 20 servings.

Tip
When making layered gelatin salads, don't wait too long before adding the next layer, or layers will slide off one another when the salad is cut and served.

Neptune's Heavenly Garden Salad

Crabmeat can be expensive, so reserve this recipe for a special family occasion or for your favorite company.

Crabmeat Dressing, see below
1 head iceberg or other lettuce
Assorted chilled fresh or canned
   vegetables, see below

Hard-cooked egg halves, if desired

Crabmeat Dressing:
1 cup mayonnaise
1/4 cup sweet pickle relish
1-1/2 tablespoons lemon juice
3 or 4 drops hot-pepper sauce

1/2 cup whipping cream, whipped
1/2 lb. fresh or thawed frozen crabmeat
2 hard-cooked eggs, chopped
2 green onions, finely chopped

Prepare Crabmeat Dressing; refrigerate. About 1 hour before serving, break lettuce into bite-size pieces; place in a large salad bowl. Cover; refrigerate. Arrange assorted vegetables and egg halves, if desired, around edge of a large platter, leaving center open. Cover; refrigerate. Just before serving, place bowl of Crabmeat Dressing in center of platter. Serve salad buffet-style, beginning with lettuce, adding desired vegetables and ending with dressing. Makes 4 to 6 servings.

Crabmeat Dressing:

In a medium bowl, combine all dressing ingredients. Cover; refrigerate at least 2 hours or up to 24 hours. Makes about 2 cups.

Suggested vegetables:

Alfalfa sprouts; cooked or canned artichoke hearts or bottoms; cooked, chilled asparagus spears; avocado slices; garbanzo beans (chick peas); sliced pickled beets; julienne-sliced raw or blanched carrots; cherry tomatoes.

Pretzel-Crust Salad

This salad is sweet enough to serve as a dessert.

2 cups crushed pretzels
1/2 cup butter or margarine, melted
1 tablespoon sugar
1 (8-oz.) pkg. cream cheese,
   room temperature
1 cup sugar

1 (8-oz.) carton frozen whipped topping,
   thawed
1 (6-oz.) pkg. strawberry-flavored gelatin
2 cups boiling water
2 (10-oz.) pkgs. frozen strawberries,
   thawed, undrained

Preheat oven to 400F (205C). In a medium bowl, combine pretzels, melted butter or margarine and 1 tablespoon sugar. Blend well, then press mixture evenly over bottom of a 13'' x 9'' baking dish. Bake 6 to 8 minutes or until firm. Do not overbake. Cool on a rack. In a medium bowl, beat cream cheese and 1 cup sugar until blended. Fold in whipped topping. Spread over cooled pretzel crust. Cover; refrigerate. In another medium bowl, combine gelatin and boiling water; stir until gelatin is dissolved. Stir in undrained strawberries. Cover; refrigerate until mixture is thickened and very syrupy. Pour mixture carefully over cream-cheese filling. Cover; refrigerate at least 6 hours or until firm, or up to 24 hours. Cut in squares to serve. Makes about 15 servings.

Chicken Reuben

This surprising combination has become a real favorite.

**4 whole chicken breasts, split,
  skinned, boned**
1 (16-oz.) jar sauerkraut, rinsed, drained

8 (1-oz.) Swiss-cheese slices
1 (16-oz.) bottle Thousand Island dressing

Arrange chicken breasts in a large, shallow baking dish. Top with sauerkraut, cheese slices and Thousand Island dressing. If preparing ahead, refrigerate uncooked chicken and toppings separately up to 24 hours; assemble casserole just before baking. To serve, cover and bake in a 350F (175C) oven, about 1 hour (1-1/4 hours if ingredients are refrigerated) or until chicken is no longer pink when slashed in thickest part. Makes 6 to 8 servings.

Yakitori Chicken Fillets

Japanese-style white rice and fresh fruit complete this Oriental meal.

**3 whole chicken breasts, split,
  skinned, boned**
1-1/2 cups soy sauce
6 green onions, thinly sliced
1 cup chicken broth

1/3 cup sugar
3 tablespoons sesame seeds, toasted
2 tablespoons grated fresh gingerroot
1/8 teaspoon pepper
1 cup thinly sliced mushrooms, if desired

Arrange chicken breasts in an 11'' x 7'' baking dish. In a medium bowl, combine remaining ingredients; pour over chicken. Cover; refrigerate at least 2 to 3 hours or up to 24 hours. To cook, preheat a grill. Lift chicken from marinade; drain over dish. Reserve marinade for sauce, if desired — see Variation, below. Place chicken on hot grill. Cook 6 to 8 minutes per side or until meat is no longer pink when slashed in thickest part. Makes 4 to 6 servings.

Variation
To serve chicken with sauce, combine marinade and 2 tablespoons cornstarch in a medium saucepan. Heat, stirring constantly, until thickened.

Avocado-Chicken Bake

This attractive company entree features a delectable combination of flavors.

1/4 cup butter or margarine
4 whole chicken breasts, split,
   skinned, boned
3 tablespoons butter or margarine
1/4 lb. fresh mushrooms, sliced
6 tablespoons all-purpose flour
1-1/2 cups half and half
1-1/2 cups chicken broth

1/2 teaspoon salt
1/8 teaspoon black pepper
1/2 cup freshly grated Parmesan cheese
   (1-1/2 oz.)
3 drops hot-pepper sauce
3/4 teaspoon dried leaf basil, crushed
1/2 cup slivered almonds, toasted
1 or 2 avocados

In a large skillet, melt 1/4 cup butter or margarine. Add chicken breasts; sauté 5 minutes on each side or until meat is no longer pink when slashed in thickest part. Remove chicken from skillet; place in a single layer in a 13'' x 9'' baking dish. Melt 3 tablespoons butter or margarine in skillet. Add mushrooms; sauté 2 to 3 minutes or until tender. Stir flour into skillet; cook, stirring, 1 minute. Slowly add half and half and broth, stirring until smooth and thickened. Stir in salt, black pepper, cheese, hot-pepper sauce and basil. Spoon sauce over chicken. If prepared ahead, cover unbaked-sauce covered chicken; refrigerate up to 24 hours. To serve, bake, uncovered, in a 350F (175C) oven, 25 to 35 minutes (35 to 40 minutes if refrigerated). Top with toasted almonds. Bake 10 more minutes or until sauce is bubbling and heated through. Pit and peel avocados. Slice lengthwise; place around edge of baking dish. Bake as directed above 35 to 40 minutes. Makes 6 to 8 servings.

Variation
Cook 1 (16-oz.) package linguine according to package directions; drain. Serve Avocado-Chicken Bake over hot cooked linguine.

Sour-Cream Chicken

If time doesn't permit refrigerating this dish 4 hours, you may bake it immediately; the flavor will be almost as good.

3 whole chicken breasts, split, boned
1/2 pint dairy sour cream (1 cup)

1/2 teaspoon garlic salt
17 round or oval butter crackers, crushed

Arrange chicken breasts in a shallow baking dish. In a small bowl, stir together sour cream and garlic salt. Spoon mixture over chicken. Sprinkle with crushed crackers. Cover; refrigerate at least 4 hours or up to 24 hours. To serve, bake chicken, uncovered, in a 325F (165C) oven, about 50 minutes or until meat is no longer pink when slashed in thickest part. Makes 4 to 6 servings.

Herbed-Chicken Foil Dinner

You can easily increase the proportions of this recipe to make additional dinners for freezer storage.

1 chicken-breast half, skinned, boned
1/8 teaspoon fines herbes
Salt and pepper to taste

1 small green onion, chopped
3 fresh broccoli spears
1 small carrot, thinly sliced

Cut an 18'' x 12'' piece of heavy foil; set aside. Place chicken breast between 2 sheets of plastic wrap. Pound with a flat-surfaced meat mallet until 1/4 inch thick, being careful not to tear meat. Place chicken breast in center of lower half of foil. Sprinkle with fines herbes, salt and pepper. Place green onion, broccoli and carrot on top of meat. Fold upper edge of foil over ingredients to meet bottom edge. Turn foil edges to form a 1/2-inch fold. Smooth fold. Double over again, and press very tightly to seal, allowing room for expansion and heat circulation. Repeat folding and sealing at each end. If preparing ahead, refrigerate unbaked packet up to 24 hours. To serve, place packet on a baking sheet; bake in a 425F (220C) oven, 20 to 25 minutes (25 to 30 minutes if refrigerated) or until chicken is no longer pink when slashed in thickest part and vegetables are tender-crisp. Makes 1 serving.

Variation
To prepare packet for freezing, blanch broccoli and carrot in boiling water 3 minutes. Remove from boiling water; plunge into cold water to cool. Drain; add to foil packet. Freeze up to 3 months. Bake frozen 30 to 35 minutes.

Low-Cal Chicken-Breast Foil Dinner

Try this on your next camping trip — or your next diet.

1 thin onion slice
1 chicken-breast half, skinned, boned
Salt and pepper to taste
1/8 teaspoon dried leaf basil, crushed

1/8 teaspoon garlic powder
1 small zucchini, thinly sliced
3 fresh mushrooms, thinly sliced
Paprika, if desired
1 teaspoon grated Parmesan cheese, if desired

Cut an 18'' x 12'' piece of heavy foil; place onion in center of lower half of foil. Place chicken breast between 2 sheets of plastic wrap. Pound with a flat-surfaced meat mallet until 1/4 inch thick, being careful not to tear meat. Place chicken breast on top of onion; sprinkle with salt, pepper, basil and garlic powder. Place zucchini and mushrooms on top of meat; sprinkle with paprika and cheese, if desired. Fold upper edge of foil over ingredients to meet bottom edge. Turn foil edges to form a 1/2-inch fold. Smooth fold. Double over again and press very tightly to seal, allowing room for expansion and heat circulation. Repeat folding and sealing at each end. If preparing ahead, refrigerate unbaked packet up to 24 hours. To serve, place packet on a baking sheet; bake in a 425F (220C) oven, 20 to 25 minutes or until chicken is no longer pink when slashed in thickest part and zucchini is tender-crisp. Makes 1 serving.

Variation
To prepare packet for freezing, blanch zucchini in boiling water 30 seconds. Remove from boiling water; plunge into cold water to cool. Drain, add to foil packet. Freeze up to 3 months. Bake frozen 30 to 35 minutes.

How to Make Hot Pizza Boats

1/Cut off and reserve a thin slice from top of each roll. Hollow out each roll, leaving a 1/4-inch-thick shell.

2/Fill rolls as directed. Replace tops on rolls; wrap each in foil. Bake until heated through.

Hot Pizza Boats

Keep in the freezer and serve to your hungry teens or Little Leaguers for "after-hours" meals. For a quick microwave lunch, rewrap frozen rolls in plastic wrap and microwave each on HIGH (100%) for 1-1/2 minutes.

1 lb. lean ground beef
1/2 cup chopped onion
1 (8-oz.) can pizza sauce
1/4 cup chopped black olives, or
  more if desired

1/2 teaspoon dried leaf oregano, crushed
1 teaspoon dried leaf basil, crushed
Pepper to taste
4 (8-inch-long) French rolls
1 cup shredded mozzarella cheese (4 oz.)

Cut 8 (12'' x 8'') pieces of foil; set aside. Crumble beef into a medium skillet. Add onion; cook, stirring, until meat is browned. Drain off fat. Stir in pizza sauce, olives, oregano, basil and pepper. Continue to cook until heated through. Remove from heat; set aside. Cut each roll in half crosswise to make 4-inch-long rolls (8 total). Cut off and reserve a thin slice from top of each roll. Hollow out each roll, leaving a 1/4-inch-thick shell. Sprinkle 1 tablespoon cheese in bottom of each roll. Spoon meat mixture over cheese. Sprinkle 1 tablespoon cheese over meat mixture. Replace tops on roll; wrap each filled roll half in 1 piece of foil. If preparing ahead, refrigerate unbaked packets up to 24 hours or freeze up to 3 months. To serve, bake in a 375F (190C) oven, 20 to 25 minutes (25 to 30 minutes if refrigerated; 35 to 40 minutes if frozen) or until cheese is melted and meat is heated through. Makes 8 servings.

Marinated London Broil

Here's a good way to make a less-tender cut of meat taste like the more expensive cuts.

**3 lbs. beef top round steak,
   2 to 2-1/2 inches thick
1/4 cup vegetable oil
1/2 cup ketchup**

**2 tablespoons white-wine tarragon vinegar
1/2 teaspoon salt
Dash of pepper
1 garlic clove, crushed**

Place steak in a shallow marinating container or dish. In a small bowl, combine oil, ketchup, vinegar, salt, pepper and garlic. Pour over steak. Cover; refrigerate at least 4 hours or up to 24 hours, turning occasionally. Preheat oven broiler. Lift meat from dish; drain, reserving marinade. Place meat on a broiler pan. Broil about 5 inches below heat source, turning frequently, 20 to 25 minutes for medium or until done to your liking. To serve, cut meat diagonally into very thin slices. In a small saucepan, bring marinade to a boil; serve over sliced steak. Makes 6 servings.

Variation
If desired, cook meat on a hot grill. Increase cooking time to 25 to 30 minutes for medium.

Tip
If you don't have a marinating container, place marinade ingredients in a plastic bag with a zip seal. Add meat; seal bag. Refrigerate as directed, turning frequently.

Beef-Broccoli Stir-Fry

This colorful dish will surely become a favorite in your home, as it is in ours.

**1 lb. beef flank steak, partially frozen
5 tablespoons soy sauce
1/4 cup cornstarch
5 tablespoons vegetable oil
1 teaspoon grated fresh gingerroot**

**2 cups uncooked long-grain white rice
2 cups beef broth
1/4 cup oyster sauce
6 cups cubed broccoli (1-1/2-inch pieces)
1/4 cup water**

Cut partially frozen steak across grain, diagonally, into thin slices. Cut slices in 1-1/2'' x 1/4'' strips. In a medium bowl, combine 3 tablespoons soy sauce, 2 tablespoons cornstarch, 2 tablespoons oil and gingerroot. Stir in meat strips. Cover; refrigerate 4 to 6 hours or up to 24 hours. About 25 to 30 minutes before serving, cook rice according to package directions. In a medium bowl, stir together broth, remaining 2 tablespoons soy sauce, remaining 2 tablespoons cornstarch and oyster sauce; set aside. In a wok or large skillet, heat 2 tablespoons remaining oil over high heat. Add broccoli; cook, stirring quickly and frequently, 4 to 5 minutes or until bright green and tender-crisp. Stir in water. Cover; continue to cook 3 more minutes. Transfer broccoli to a bowl; set aside. Heat remaining 1 tablespoon oil in wok over high heat. Add meat mixture; cook 4 to 5 minutes, stirring frequently. Reduce heat. Add broccoli. Stir through broth mixture; add to wok. Continue to cook, stirring, 4 to 5 more minutes or until sauce thickens and meat is done. Serve over hot rice. Makes 6 servings.

Cathy's German Sauerbraten with Gingersnap Gravy

Serve with potato pancakes or dumplings.

2 medium onions, sliced
1 lemon, sliced
2-1/2 cups water
1 tablespoon sugar
1 tablespoon salt
1-1/2 cups red-wine vinegar

12 whole cloves
6 bay leaves
6 whole peppercorns
1 teaspoon ground ginger
1 (4- to 5-lb.) beef rump roast
2 tablespoons vegetable shortening
Gingersnap Gravy, see below

Gingersnap Gravy:
2-1/4 cups meat cooking liquid
   (reserved from cooking roast)

3/4 cup water
1 cup broken gingersnaps

In a large marinating container or bowl, combine onions, lemon, water, sugar, salt, vinegar, cloves, bay leaves, peppercorns and ginger. Add roast, turning to coat. Cover; refrigerate 3 to 4 days, turning occasionally and spooning marinade over beef so it absorbs flavor evenly. Remove beef from marinade; pat dry with paper towels. Strain and reserve marinade. In a large Dutch oven, melt shortening over medium-high heat. Add meat; cook until browned on all sides. Add strained marinade. Reduce heat until mixture barely simmers. Cover; simmer 2 to 2-1/2 hours or until tender, turning meat occasionally. Remove meat to a platter; reserve cooking liquid. Prepare Gingersnap Gravy. Cut meat into thin slices; serve with gravy. Makes 8 to 10 servings.

Gingersnap Gravy:
Skim and discard fat from reserved meat cooking liquid. Discard bay leaves. Pour 2-1/4 cups skimmed cooking liquid into a medium saucepan. Add water and broken gingersnaps. Cook over low heat until thick, stirring frequently.

Best-Ever Barbecued Spareribs

Cooking ahead, then marinating overnight, makes these tender, mouthwatering ribs the best ever.

4 to 5 lbs. country-style pork spareribs
Barbecue Basting Sauce, see below

Barbecue Basting Sauce:
1 cup sparerib broth (reserve
   from cooking spareribs)
1 cup bottled barbecue sauce

2/3 cup honey
1/2 cup soy sauce
1/4 cup tomato paste

Place spareribs in a large Dutch oven. Add just enough water to cover. Bring to a boil over high heat. Reduce heat. Cover; simmer 1-1/4 hours or until meat is no longer pink when slashed. Remove ribs from broth; place in a shallow baking dish or marinating container. Reserve 1 cup broth. Prepare Barbecue Basting Sauce; pour over ribs in dish. Cover; refrigerate at least 4 hours or up to 24 hours, turning once. Preheat a grill. Lift ribs from sauce; drain. Place on hot grill. Cook 20 to 30 minutes, basting with sauce and turning frequently. Makes 4 to 6 servings.
Barbecue Basting Sauce:
In a medium bowl, combine 1 cup reserved broth, barbecue sauce, honey, soy sauce and tomato paste.

"The Works" Oven Stew

Take this along on your next camp-out and serve it with French bread and cold milk.

1-1/2 lbs. beef stew meat, cut in
   1-inch cubes
1 teaspoon garlic salt
1/4 teaspoon pepper
1/4 cup all-purpose flour
3 tablespoons vegetable shortening
1 large onion, chopped
3 tablespoons all-purpose flour
4 cups water
6 large carrots, peeled, cut in
   1-inch chunks

5 large potatoes, peeled, cubed
2 cups sliced celery
1 (1-3/8-oz.) pkg. dry onion soup mix
1 (10-3/4-oz.) can cream of mushroom soup
1 tablespoon Worcestershire sauce
1 bay leaf
1/8 teaspoon ground thyme
1/8 teaspoon ground marjoram
1-1/2 cups fresh or frozen green peas

Place beef in a large bowl; sprinkle with garlic salt, pepper and 1/4 cup flour. Toss to coat. In a Dutch oven, melt shortening over medium-high heat. Add coated meat; cook until browned on all sides. Stir in onion; continue to cook until onion is tender but not browned. In a small bowl, combine 3 tablespoons flour with 1 cup water. Blend until smooth. Add to meat mixture with remaining 3 cups water. Add carrots, potatoes, celery, onion soup mix, cream of mushroom soup, Worcestershire sauce, bay leaf, thyme and marjoram. Cook, stirring, until thickened. Cover and bake in a 350F (175C) oven, about 3 hours or until meat is tender. Stir in peas; continue to bake 15 more minutes. Makes 8 to 10 servings.

Tip
To take oven stew on a camp-out, wrap in a large beach towel after removing from oven. Place beach-towel-wrapped Dutch oven in a brown-paper grocery bag; staple shut. The stew will stay hot for several hours without reheating.

Pork & Squash Foil Dinner

Brown sugar and honey make a syrup that bastes the pork chop and enhances the flavor.

1 medium pork chop, 1 inch thick
1/8 teaspoon salt
Dash of pepper
3 (1/2-inch-thick) slices acorn squash

1 tablespoon butter or margarine
1 tablespoon brown sugar
1 tablespoon honey

Cut an 18'' x 12'' piece of heavy foil; place pork chop in center of lower half of foil. Sprinkle with salt and pepper. Lay squash slices on top of chop. Dot butter or margarine in center of each slice. Sprinkle with brown sugar; drizzle with honey. Fold upper edge of foil over ingredients to meet bottom edge. Turn foil edges to form a 1/2-inch fold. Smooth fold. Double over again; press very tightly to seal, allowing room for expansion and heat circulation. Repeat folding and sealing at each end. If preparing ahead, refrigerate up to 24 hours or freeze up to 3 months. To serve, place packet on a baking sheet; bake in a 425F (220C) oven, 25 to 30 minutes (30 to 35 minutes if refrigerated; 35 to 45 minutes if frozen) or until chop and squash are tender. Makes 1 serving.

Seafood Wellington

Accompany this elegant entree with butter green beans and boiled new potatoes.

1 (10-oz.) pkg. frozen patty shells
(6 patty shells), thawed
6 (3- to 4-oz.) sole fillets, patted dry
Salt and pepper to taste

1/4 teaspoon dried leaf tarragon, crushed
1 egg
1 tablespoon water
Sauce Béarnaise, page 125

Grease a baking sheet; set aside. Place 1 thawed patty shell between 2 sheets of floured wax paper. Roll out to a circle about 7 inches in diameter. Repeat with remaining 5 patty shells to make a total of 6 circles. Pat fillets dry with paper towels; sprinkle each with salt, pepper and tarragon. Fold fillets in half; place 1 folded fillet in center of each pastry circle. In a small bowl beat egg and water. Lightly wet pastry edge. Bring pastry up around fillet to cover completely. Remove any excess pastry; reserve to use for decorative cutouts. Pinch seams to seal. Place each pastry packet, seam-side down, on greased baking sheet. Brush some of egg mixture over each packet, being careful not to let egg drip down sides of packets. Place reserved pastry scraps between 2 sheets of floured wax paper; roll out. Cut 12 leaf shapes or make free form designs from rolled-out pastry. Place 2 leaves or free form designs on each pastry packet. Brush design with egg mixture. Cover with plastic wrap; refrigerate at least 30 minutes or up to 24 hours. Preheat oven to 400F (205C). Bake 25 to 30 minutes or until golden brown. Just before packets are done, prepare Sauce Béarnaise; pour into a serving container and pass at table. Makes 6 servings.

Seafood Wellington

How to Make Red-Snapper Foil Dinner

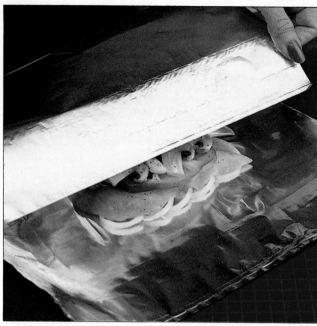

1/On each piece of foil, layer ingredients. Fold foil over layered ingredients, so foil edges meet.

2/Turn foil edges to form a 1/2-inch fold; smooth fold. Double over again; press very tightly to seal. Repeat fold with edges of packet to enclose fish completely.

Red-Snapper Foil Dinner

The fish lover of the family is sure to enjoy this colorful snapper-and-vegetable dinner.

1 onion slice
1/4 lb. red snapper fillet
1 green bell pepper slice
3 fresh mushrooms, thinly sliced

Salt and black pepper to taste
2 teaspoons butter or margarine
1 tomato slice
1/4 cup shredded Cheddar cheese (1 oz.)

Cut an 18'' x 12'' piece of heavy foil; place onion in center of lower half of foil. Place red snapper on top of onion; top with bell pepper. Add mushrooms; sprinkle with salt and black pepper. Dot with butter or margarine. Fold upper edge of foil over ingredients to meet bottom edge. Turn foil edges to form a 1/2-inch fold. Smooth fold. Double over again and press very tightly to seal, allowing room for expansion and heat circulation. Repeat folding and sealing at each end. If preparing ahead, refrigerate unbaked packet up to 24 hours. To serve, place packet on a baking sheet; bake in a 425F (220C) oven, 20 minutes (25 to 30 minutes if refrigerated). Open packet; add tomato. Rewrap and continue to bake 5 more minutes or until fish is flaky and opaque throughout. Remove from oven; unwrap and top with cheese. Serve immediately. Complete baking as directed above. Makes 1 serving.

Variation

To prepare packet for freezing, use only fresh fish. Prepare as above. Freeze up to 3 months. Bake frozen 30 to 35 minutes; then unwrap and add tomato. Continue to bake 5 more minutes. Unwrap; top with cheese.

No-Fail Cheese Soufflé

Check the Leftover Encyclopedia, page 126, for uses for reserved bread crusts.

12 slices day-old white bread
3 cups shredded Cheddar cheese (12 oz.)
3/4 lb. country-style pork sausage,
    cooked, drained
5 eggs
2-1/2 cups milk

3/4 teaspoon salt
1/2 teaspoon dry mustard
1/4 teaspoon paprika
1/2 teaspoon Worcestershire sauce
1/3 cup butter or margarine, melted

Butter a 2-quart casserole dish or soufflé dish. Remove crusts from bread; reserve crusts for another use. Cut trimmed bread slices in 1/2-inch cubes. Layer 1/3 of the bread cubes, 1/3 of the cheese and 1/3 of the sausage in buttered dish. Repeat layers 2 more times. In a medium bowl, beat together eggs, milk, salt, mustard, paprika and Worcestershire sauce. Slowly pour over bread, cheese and sausage. Pour melted butter or margarine over top. Cover; refrigerate at least 8 hours or up to 24 hours. Remove from refrigerator 30 minutes to 1 hour before baking. Preheat oven to 350F (175C). Uncover casserole and place in a baking pan. Pour boiling water into pan until water level is 1 inch up side of casserole. Bake 1-1/4 hours or until golden brown and set. Makes 6 servings.

Foil Side Dishes

These vegetable side dishes make handy accompaniments to many meals.

Vegetable and seasoning combinations
    as desired, see below

Cut a 12-inch-square piece of heavy foil. Place desired vegetable combination on foil. Sprinkle with seasonings. Fold upper edge of foil over ingredients to meet bottom edge. Turn foil edges to form a 1/2-inch fold. Smooth fold. Double over again and press very tightly to seal, allowing room for expansion and heat circulation. Repeat folding and sealing at each end. If preparing ahead, refrigerate unbaked packet up to 24 hours. To serve, place packet on a baking sheet; bake in a 425F (220C) oven, 20 to 25 minutes (25 to 30 minutes if refrigerated) or until vegetables are tender-crisp. Makes 1 serving.

Variation

To prepare packet for freezing, blanch all root and firm vegetables in boiling water 3 minutes. Blanch zucchini and other vegetables only 30 seconds to 1 minute. *Do not* blanch mushrooms. Remove blanched vegetables from boiling water; plunge into cold water to cool. Drain; package in foil as directed. Freeze up to 3 months. Bake frozen 30 to 35 minutes.

Suggested vegetable and seasoning combinations:

Yellow squash slices, fresh mushroom slices, dried leaf basil; broccoli spears, cauliflowerets, salt and pepper, dot of butter or sprinkling of grated cheese; edible pea pods, sliced carrots, salt and pepper.

Twice-Baked Potatoes

Nevada's family agrees that twice-baking makes these twice as good as regular baked potatoes.

12 large baking potatoes
1 to 1-1/2 cups milk
1/2 cup butter or margarine, cubed
1 teaspoon salt

1/2 teaspoon seasoned salt
1/8 teaspoon garlic powder
1/4 teaspoon pepper
1-1/2 cups shredded Cheddar cheese (6 oz.)

Scrub potatoes well; prick each with a fork in several places. Place potatoes directly on oven racks. Bake in a 375F (190C) oven, 1 to 1-1/4 hours or until tender when pierced with a fork. Cut a thin slice from top of each potato. Scoop out insides, leaving a thin shell. Place scooped-out potato flesh in a large bowl; mash until no lumps remain. Add 1 cup milk; beat until smooth. Beat in up to 1/2 cup more milk, if desired, to make potatoes fluffier. Add butter or margarine, salt, seasoned salt, garlic powder and pepper. Beat vigorously until mixture is light and fluffy. Fill potato shells with beaten potato mixture. Sprinkle 2 tablespoons cheese on each filled potato. If preparing ahead, wrap potatoes in foil and freeze up to 1 month. To serve, place potatoes on a baking sheet; unwrap frozen potatoes. Bake 20 minutes (40 to 45 minutes) or until center of potatoes are heated through and cheese has melted. Serve immediately. Makes 12 servings.

Mashed-Potato Delight

Cottage cheese, grated onion and a sprinkling of almonds give mashed potatoes a new look — and taste!

4 cups mashed potatoes
   (6 large baking potatoes)
1 teaspoon salt
16 ozs. cream-style cottage cheese (2 cups)
3/4 cup dairy sour cream

1-1/2 tablespoons grated onion
1/8 teaspoon pepper
1/4 cup butter or margarine, melted
1/3 cup sliced almonds

In a large bowl, combine potatoes, salt, cottage cheese, sour cream, onion and pepper. Spoon into an ungreased 2-quart casserole dish. Pour melted butter or margarine over potato mixture; sprinkle with almonds. If prepared ahead, cover unbaked casserole; refrigerate up to 24 hours. To serve, stir in butter or margarine. Cover and bake in a 375F (190C) oven, 45 to 50 minutes (50 to 55 minutes if refrigerated) or until heated through. Makes 6 to 8 servings.

Holiday Sweet-Potato-Walnut Puffs

This do-ahead dish will make preparing your holiday feast a little easier.

8 canned pineapple slices
1 (29-oz.) can sweet potatoes or yams
2 tablespoons pineapple juice
3 tablespoons packed brown sugar
1 tablespoon butter or margarine,
   room temperature

1/4 teaspoon ground nutmeg
1/8 teaspoon salt
About 3 tablespoons chopped walnuts
40 miniature marshmallows or
   8 large marshmallows

Grease a 13'' x 9'' baking dish. Place pineapple slices in a single layer in greased baking dish; set aside. In a medium bowl, beat sweet potatoes or yams with an electric mixer until smooth. In a small bowl, combine pineapple juice, brown sugar, butter or margarine, nutmeg and salt. Stir into sweet potatoes. Using an ice cream scoop, scoop out sweet-potato mixture, placing 1 scoop atop each pineapple slice. Sprinkle evenly with walnuts. If preparing ahead, cover unbaked sweet-potato-topped pineapple mounds. Refrigerate up to 24 hours. To serve, bake, uncovered, in a 350F (175C) oven, 20 minutes (25 minutes if refrigerated). Remove from oven; top each puff with 5 miniature marshmallows or 1 large marshmallow. Return to oven; continue to bake about 7 more minutes or until marshmallows are melted and golden brown. Makes 8 servings.

Whipped-Cream Biscuits

These are a wonderful accompaniment to hot stews and homemade soups.

2 cups all-purpose flour
4 teaspoons baking powder
1-1/2 teaspoons sugar
3/4 teaspoon salt

1/2 pint whipping cream (1 cup)
1 to 2 tablespoons milk
3 tablespoons butter or margarine, melted

In a large bowl, stir together flour, baking powder, sugar and salt. Stir in cream and 1 tablespoon milk to make a soft dough. If mixture is too dry, add about 1 more tablespoon milk. On a lightly floured surface, gently knead dough 10 times or until it holds together. Roll out about 1/2 inch thick. Cut out dough with a round 2-inch biscuit cutter. Dip floured side of cutouts in melted butter or margarine. Place, buttered-side up, on an ungreased baking sheet. If preparing ahead, cover unbaked biscuits with plastic wrap; refrigerate up to 24 hours. To serve, bake in a preheated 425F (220C) oven, 14 to 16 minutes or until golden brown. Serve hot. Makes about 12 biscuits.

Tip
Re-rolled biscuit dough sometimes produces tough biscuits. To avoid this problem, let dough scraps rest in the refrigerator for about 10 minutes until flour is absorbed. Then re-roll.

Onion-Bread Spread

Keep on hand for quick onion bread.

**1/2 cup butter or margarine,
  room temperature**
2 tablespoons Worcestershire sauce

1 medium onion, grated
1 cup mayonnaise

In a medium bowl, combine butter or margarine, Worcestershire sauce, onion and mayonnaise. Stir until blended. If preparing ahead, cover and refrigerate up to 1 month. Makes about 1-1/2 cups.

To make Gourmet Onion Bread:
**1 loaf Italian or French bread,
  cut in half horizontally**
1/2 cup Onion-Bread Spread

2 tablespoons grated Parmesan cheese
Dried parsley flakes
Paprika

Preheat on oven broiler. Place bread, cut-side up, on a baking sheet. Spread Onion-Bread Spread on cut surface of bread. Sprinkle with cheese, parsley flakes and paprika. Broil about 6 inches below heat source 2 to 3 minutes or until cheese is melted and just beginning to brown. Slice diagonally; serve hot. Makes 8 to 10 servings.

Raisin-Molasses Muffins

This make-ahead batter makes breakfast a breeze.

1 cup quick-cooking rolled oats
2 cups whole-bran cold cereal
1 cup boiling water
2 cups buttermilk
3/4 cup packed brown sugar
3/4 cup light molasses
2-1/2 cups all-purpose flour
1 tablespoon baking soda

1 teaspoon salt
1 teaspoon ground cinnamon
1/4 teaspoon ground cloves
1/4 teaspoon ground nutmeg
1/2 cup vegetable oil
2 eggs
1 cup raisins
1/2 cup chopped walnuts

Grease about 36 muffin cups. In a large bowl, combine oats and whole-bran cereal. Stir in boiling water and buttermilk. Stir in brown sugar and molasses until all ingredients are blended; set aside. In a medium bowl, combine flour, baking soda, salt, cinnamon, cloves and nutmeg; set aside. Add oil and eggs to bran mixture, stirring until blended. Gradually stir in flour mixture. Stir just until all ingredients are moistened. Fold in raisins and nuts. Fill greased muffin cups 2/3 full. If preparing ahead, pour unbaked batter into a container with a tight-fitting lid. Cover tightly; refrigerate up to 1 week. To serve, bake in a 375F (190C) oven, 20 to 25 minutes (25 to 30 minutes if refrigerated) or until tops spring back when lightly touched. Turn out of pans and place on racks to cool. Makes about 36 muffins.

Overnight Basic Buttermilk Dough

We thank Karine's mother-in-law for this favorite recipe. The dough keeps in the refrigerator for up to a week.

3 cups buttermilk
3 cups all-purpose flour
1 (1/4-oz.) envelope active dry yeast
   (1 tablespoon)
1/2 cup sugar

1/2 cup vegetable oil
3 eggs, beaten
2 teaspoons salt
1 teaspoon baking soda
5 to 6 cups all-purpose flour

In a medium saucepan, heat buttermilk to 110F (45C). Pour into a large bowl. Stir in 3 cups flour, yeast and sugar. Let stand 1 hour. Add oil, eggs, salt, baking soda and 5 to 6 cups flour to make a soft dough. Cover; let rise in a warm place 30 minutes. Cover and refrigerate at least 8 hours or up to 1 week. Three to four hours before serving, shape dough into desired types of rolls as directed below. Cover shaped dough; let rise 2 to 4 hours or until doubled in bulk. Bake as directed below for individual types of rolls. Makes 36 to 48 rolls.

Parker House Rolls: Lightly grease 2 baking sheets. Roll out dough about 1/2 inch thick. Cut into 2-1/2-inch circles. Dip 1 side of each circle in melted butter or margarine; fold in half so buttered surfaces are together and top half overlaps bottom half slightly. Place rolls close together on greased baking sheets. Cover and let rise 2 to 4 hours or until doubled in bulk. Bake in a 375F (190C) oven, 15 to 20 minutes or until golden brown. Makes 36 rolls.

Crescent Rolls: Lightly grease 2 baking sheets. Divide dough into 3 equal portions. Roll out each portion to a 10- to 12-inch circle. Cut each circle into 12 wedges. Roll up wedges, beginning at wide end. Place rolls with points underneath on greased baking sheets. Cover; let rise 2 to 4 hours or until doubled in bulk. Bake in a 400F (205C) oven, 10 to 15 minutes or until golden brown. Makes 36 rolls.

Orange Crescent Rolls: Follow directions for Crescent Rolls, but spread Orange Filling, below, on dough circles before cutting and rolling. Glaze with Orange Glaze, below, after baking.

   Orange Filling: In a small bowl, combine 3 tablespoons melted butter or margarine, 2 tablespoons grated orange peel, 3 tablespoons orange juice and 3/4 cup sugar.

   Orange Glaze: In a small bowl, combine 2 cups powdered sugar and 3 to 4 tablespoons orange juice.

Caramel-Pecan Rolls: In a small bowl, combine 3/4 cup melted butter or margarine, 1 cup packed brown sugar and 3 tablespoons light corn syrup. Divide mixture evenly among 36 muffin cups. Sprinkle about 1 teaspoon broken pecans into each cup. Divide dough in half. Roll out each half to a 12'' x 6'' rectangle about 1/2 inch thick. Brush each half with 2 tablespoons melted butter or margarine; sprinkle lightly with ground cinnamon. Roll up jelly-roll style, starting with a long end. Cut each roll into 18 (about 3/4-inch-thick) slices. Place slices, cut-side down, in prepared muffin cups. Cover; let rise 2 to 4 hours or until doubled in bulk. Bake in a 375F (190C) oven, 12 to 15 minutes or until golden brown. Invert rolls from muffin cups onto racks. Makes 36 rolls.

Soft Breadsticks: Lightly grease 2 or 3 baking sheets. Divide dough into 36 balls. Roll each ball between your palms to form a rope about 1/2 inch thick and 6 to 8 inches long. Place ropes about 1 inch apart on greased baking sheets. Cover; let rise 1 to 2 hours. Beat 1 egg with a fork; brush each breadstick with beaten egg. Sprinkle with sesame seeds, if desired. Bake in a 400F (205C) oven, 12 to 15 minutes or until golden brown. Makes 36 breadsticks.

Fried Scones: Roll out dough about 1/4 inch thick. Cut into rectangles about 4'' x 2''. Cover; let rise 30 minutes. In a medium skillet, heat about 1 inch of oil to 375F (190C) or until a 1-inch bread cube turns golden brown in about 50 seconds. Fry strips of dough, several at a time, until golden brown on the bottom. Turn with tongs; fry until other side is golden brown. Drain on paper towels. Serve hot with butter and jam or with honey-butter. Makes about 36 scones.

Our Favorite Cheesecake

Baked cheesecake has a creamier texture when the pan is placed in another shallow pan of water.

Graham-Cracker Crust, see below
4 (8-oz.) pkgs. cream cheese,
  room temperature
1-1/2 cups sugar
4 eggs, beaten
4 teaspoons vanilla extract

2 teaspoons lemon juice
2 teaspoons grated lemon peel
Sour-Cream Topping, see below
1 (21-oz.) can cherry-pie filling,
  if desired

Graham-Cracker Crust:
1/4 cup sugar
1-1/2 cups graham-cracker crumbs
  (about 18 graham cracker squares)

1/4 cup butter or margarine, melted

Sour-Cream Topping:
1/2 pint dairy sour cream (1 cup),
  room temperature

1/4 cup sugar
1 teaspoon vanilla extract

Prepare Graham-Cracker Crust; set aside. In a large bowl, beat together cream cheese, sugar, eggs, vanilla, lemon juice and lemon peel until very smooth. Set aside. Cover outside bottom of springform pan with 2 pieces of foil, crisscrossing foil pieces across pan bottom and bringing them up pan side to about 1 inch above rim. This foil wrapping prevents water from the water bath from penetrating the crust. Spoon cream-cheese mixture into baked crust. Place springform pan in another pan and add enough water to come 1 inch up side of springform pan. Place in preheated oven and bake 1 hour and 20 minutes. Meanwhile, prepare Sour-Cream Topping. Spread topping on cheesecake and continue to bake 7 to 10 more minutes or until topping is set. Remove springform pan from pan of water to a wire rack; remove foil wrapping. Cool cheesecake, then cover with plastic wrap and refrigerate at least 8 hours or up to 24 hours. To serve, remove pan side. Top cheesecake with cherry-pie filling, if desired. Makes about 15 servings.

Graham-Cracker Crust:
Preheat oven to 325F (165C). Butter bottom and side of a 9-inch springform pan. In a medium bowl, combine sugar and graham-cracker crumbs. Stir in melted butter or margarine until crumbs are evenly moistened. Press mixture evenly over bottom and up side of buttered pan. Bake 10 to 12 minutes or until golden brown. Remove pan from oven to a wire rack: cool. Do not turn off oven.

Sour-Cream Topping:
In a small bowl, combine sour cream, sugar and vanilla. Blend well.

How to Make Our Favorite Cheesecake

1/Bake crust in a springform pan; cool. Wrap outside bottom of pan with 2 pieces of foil, crisscrossed to prevent water from penetrating crust.

2/Bake as directed. Cool; cover and refrigerate until chilled. Top cheesecake with cherry-pie filling, if desired.

Southern Pound Cake

Southern pound cake was a "secret family recipe" for years — but the secret is out now, so you can make this tender pound cake for yourself.

3 cups sugar
1 cup vegetable shortening
5 eggs
1 teaspoon vanilla extract
1 teaspoon lemon extract

3 cups cake flour
1 teaspoon baking powder
Dash of salt
1 cup milk

Preheat oven to 350F (175C). Generously grease a 10-inch tube pan. In a large bowl, beat sugar and shortening with an electric mixer until fluffy. Beat in eggs, 1 at a time; continue to beat until light. Beat in vanilla and lemon extract. In a medium bowl, sift together flour, baking powder and salt. Add flour mixture to creamed mixture alternately with milk, beating after each addition until well blended. Scrape bowl often. Pour batter into greased pan. Bake 60 to 65 minutes or until a wooden pick inserted in center comes out clean. Cool in pan on a rack 15 minutes. Remove from pan; cool completely on rack. If preparing ahead, wrap cooled cake in heavy foil; freeze up to 2 months. Makes about 12 servings.

Williams' Family Birthday Cake

Spectacular to the eye and even more scrumptious to the palate!

Filling, see below
1 (18-1/4-oz.) pkg. chocolate-cake mix
1 teaspoon baking powder
3 tablespoons powdered whipped-topping mix
1/3 cup vegetable shortening

1/2 cup vegetable oil
1-1/4 cups milk
4 eggs
Frosting, see below
2 tablespoons sliced almonds, toasted

Filling:

1/2 cup milk
1 tablespoon cornstarch
2-1/2 cups sifted powdered sugar

1/2 cup vegetable shortening
1 teaspoon vanilla extract
Dash of salt

Frosting:

1 (12-oz.) carton frozen whipped topping, thawed

3/4 cup chocolate-fudge topping

Make Filling; set aside. Preheat oven to 350F (175C). Grease and flour 2 round 8-inch baking pans. In a large bowl, combine cake mix, baking powder, whipped-topping mix, shortening, oil and milk. Beat with an electric mixer on low speed until moistened. Beat in eggs, 1 at a time; beat 2 minutes on medium speed. Pour batter into prepared pans. Bake 35 to 40 minutes or until a wooden pick inserted in center comes out clean. Cool 10 minutes in pans; remove from pans. Cool completely on racks. Cut cooled cake layers in half horizontally to make a total of 4 thin layers. Place 1 layer on a cake plate. Spread 1/3 of Filling on top. Top with a second layer; spread 1/2 of remaining Filling on top. Repeat with 1 more layer and remaining Filling. Place remaining cake layer on top. Freeze cake 1 hour. Prepare Frosting. Frost cake, reserving about 3/4 cup Frosting for garnish. Return cake to freezer. Put reserved Frosting in a pastry bag fitted with a No. 32 tip; refrigerate 1/2 to 1 hour. Place toasted almonds in center of cake. Pipe chilled Frosting around top and bottom of cake in a decorative design. If preparing ahead, place cake in an airtight cake container; freeze up to 1 month. Remove 30 to 45 minutes before serving. If serving that day, return cake to freezer; remove 20 to 30 minutes before serving. Makes 10 to 12 servings.

Filling:

In a small saucepan, combine milk and cornstarch. Cook over medium-high heat until thickened, stirring frequently. Remove from heat; cool. In a medium bowl, combine 1 cup powdered sugar and shortening. Beat with an electric mixer until creamy. Add cooled cornstarch mixture; beat in remaining 1-1/2 cups powdered sugar. Beat in vanilla and salt.

Frosting:

In a medium bowl, carefully fold together whipped topping and chocolate-fudge topping with a spoon.

Chocolate Charlotte

Looks like you worked for hours, but it's easy to prepare.

2 (4-oz.) bars sweet baking chocolate,
  broken into small pieces
1/4 cup water
3 eggs, separated
2 tablespoons powdered sugar

1 (8-oz.) carton frozen whipped topping,
  thawed
12 to 24 whole ladyfingers, split
Shaved unsweetened or semisweet chocolate,
  if desired

Melt sweet baking chocolate in the top of a double boiler over simmering water, stirring constantly. Beat in water, egg yolks and powdered sugar. Remove from heat; cool. In a large bowl, beat egg whites until stiff but not dry. Fold cooled chocolate mixture into beaten egg whites. Fold in about 2 cups whipped topping; reserve remaining topping for garnish. Line sides and bottom of a flat-bottomed, straight-sided 1-1/2-quart bowl or soufflé dish with split ladyfingers. Spoon chocolate mixture into bowl, being careful not to move ladyfingers. Cover; refrigerate at least 2 to 3 hours or up to 24 hours. Just before serving, garnish with reserved whipped topping and shaved chocolate, if desired. Makes 8 servings.

French Cream Pie

This cream-pie filling makes a nice filling for cream puffs, too.

1/2 cup sugar
1/4 cup all-purpose flour
2 tablespoons cornstarch
Pinch of salt
1 egg yolk
2-1/2 cups milk

2 teaspoons vanilla extract
1 tablespoon butter or margarine
1 (9-inch) baked pastry shell, page 53
1/2 pint whipping cream (1 cup), whipped,
  sweetened

In a heavy saucepan, stir together sugar, flour, cornstarch and salt. In a small bowl, combine egg yolk and 1/2 cup milk. Stir into flour mixture until smooth. Using a whisk, gradually stir in remaining 2 cups milk. Stirring constantly, bring to a boil over medium-high heat. Remove from heat; stir in vanilla and butter or margarine. Cool 5 minutes. Pour into pastry shell. Cover with plastic wrap; refrigerate until cold or up to 24 hours. To serve, remove plastic wrap; top with whipped cream. Makes 6 to 8 servings.

Variations
Cream-Puff Filling: Prepare filling as directed above, omitting sugar from whipped cream. Fold whipped cream into completely cooled filling.
Banana Cream Pie: Slice 3 bananas into bottom of pastry shell before pouring in filling.
Coconut Cream Pie: Add 1 cup flaked coconut to filling before pouring into pastry shell. Garnish with 1/3 cup toasted flaked coconut, if desired.

Strawberry-Rum-Cream Cake

When you make an angel food cake, use this heavenly recipe to accommodate ten of the leftover egg yolks.

2 cups sifted cake flour
1-1/3 cups sugar
1 tablespoon baking powder
1 teaspoon salt
1/3 cup butter or margarine, melted, cooled
1 cup milk
1 teaspoon vanilla extract

Rum-Cream Filling:
3/4 cup sugar
3 tablespoons cornstarch
1/4 teaspoon salt
6 egg yolks (1/2 cup)

1/4 teaspoon rum extract
4 egg yolks (1/3 cup)
Rum-Cream Filling, see below
1 pint fresh strawberries, washed, stemmed
1 pint whipping cream (2 cups), whipped, sweetened
About 16 whole strawberries

3 cups milk or half and half
1 teaspoon vanilla extract
1/4 to 1/2 teaspoon rum extract

Preheat oven to 350F (175C). Generously grease and flour 2 round 8-inch baking pans. In a large bowl, sift together flour, sugar, baking powder and salt. Add melted butter or margarine, milk, vanilla and rum extract. Beat with an electric mixer 2 minutes. Add egg yolks; beat 2 more minutes. Pour into prepared pans. Bake 25 to 30 minutes or until a wooden pick inserted in center comes out clean. Cool in pans 5 minutes. Remove from pans; cool completely on racks. Prepare Rum-Cream Filling; set aside. Slice the 1 pint fresh strawberries; set aside. Cut cooled cake layers in half horizontally to make a total of 4 thin layers. Place 1 cake layer on a serving plate. Spread with about 1 cup of Rum-Cream Filling; top with 1/2 of sliced strawberries. Put a second cake layer on top; spread with about 1 cup of Rum-Cream Filling. Top with third cake layer. Spread remaining Rum-Cream Filling over this layer; cover with remaining sliced strawberries. Set last cake layer in place. Frost top and side of cake with whipped cream. If desired, reserve about 3/4 cup cream. Put in a pastry bag fitted with a No. 32 tip and pipe borders around top and bottom edge of cake. Reserve 6 whole strawberries. Cut remaining berries in half lengthwise. Place halved strawberries cut-side down around top of cake to form a circle. Cut remaining whole berries into fans and garnish cake. Refrigerate until serving time or up to 24 hours. If preparing to freeze, omit strawberry garnish. Place cake in an airtight cake container; freeze up to 1 month. Thaw at room temperature 5 to 6 hours or until completely thawed. Makes 12 to 16 servings.

Rum-Cream Filling:
In a medium saucepan, stir together sugar, cornstarch and salt. In a medium bowl, beat egg yolks and milk or half and half until blended. Place pan over medium-low heat; gradually add egg-yolk mixture, stirring constantly. Cook, stirring, until mixture is thickened and bubbly. Remove from heat; add vanilla and rum extract. Cool filling completely before assembling cake.

Strawberry-Rum-Cream Cake

Superstar Sherbet Dessert

This dessert may be served immediately or frozen for future use.

1/2 gal. raspberry sherbet
1/2 gal. pineapple sherbet
1 (10-oz.) pkg. frozen raspberries,
   thawed just enough to break apart easily
1 (12-oz.) pkg. frozen blueberries

1 (15-1/4-oz.) can crushed pineapple,
   drained
4 bananas, diced
1 cup chopped pecans

Let sherbets stand at room temperature 15 minutes to soften slightly. In a large bowl, combine sherbets just to marble. Gently fold in raspberries, blueberries, pineapple, bananas and pecans. Serve immediately. Or spoon into freezer containers; freeze up to 3 months. Remove frozen dessert from freezer 30 minutes before serving. Makes about 24 servings.

Variation
Orange-Pineapple Superstar Sherbet Dessert: Substitute orange sherbet for the raspberry sherbet. Omit the raspberries and blueberries and add 1 (11-oz.) can mandarin-orange sections, drained.

Ice-Cream Snowballs

Decorate the tops with holly leaves and berries made from colored frosting. Keep in the freezer for holiday entertaining.

1/2 gal. vanilla ice cream
2 cups shredded coconut

Purchased Chocolate Sauce

Scoop ice cream into 10 to 12 balls, working quickly so ice cream doesn't melt. Roll each ball in coconut. Place balls on an ungreased baking sheet; freeze until solid. Arrange in a single layer in an airtight container; freeze up to 3 months. Top with Chocolate Sauce at serving time. Makes 10 to 12 servings.

Lemon-Rice Pudding

Great served the traditional way as a dessert or topped with milk for breakfast.

12 eggs
2 cups sugar
3 cups milk
2 tablespoons lemon extract

1 cup raisins
6 tablespoons butter or margarine, melted
2-1/2 cups cooked long-grain white rice
Ground cinnamon

Preheat oven to 325F (165C). Butter a 13'' x 9'' baking dish. In a large bowl, combine eggs, sugar, milk, lemon extract and raisins. Beat until well blended. Stir in melted butter or margarine and rice. Pour into buttered baking dish; sprinkle with cinnamon. Bake 50 to 55 minutes or until golden brown. Serve warm. If preparing ahead, cool pudding completely; cover, refrigerate up to 24 hours and serve chilled. Makes 8 to 10 servings.

CHAPTER FIVE

Don't Throw It Away

Leftovers are a fact of life. Your refrigerator may start out "clean" on Monday, but by week's end the shelves are probably crowded with little jars and covered containers of this and that: a lone chicken leg, a cup of cooked broccoli, some wilted tossed salad, a half-can of tomato sauce. All too often, our solution to the problem of proliferating leftovers is simply to throw them out—or to ignore them until we *have* to discard them. That's not the right solution, though. Many things we throw away almost automatically can be recycled into tasty new meals or money-saving additions to our menus.

This chapter begins with a system for salvaging leftovers: the refrigerator shakedown. Using the weekly shakedown method and our Basic Nine recipes, you'll be able to convert those "unusable" scraps into one or more free meals. We also include a Leftover Encyclopedia—ideas and recipes for using typical mealtime leftovers as well as other often-wasted items, from bread crusts to vegetable cooking liquid.

We feel this chapter will create new interest in those foods that are sometimes neglected and wasted. Schedule a refrigerator shakedown weekly; review the Leftover Encyclopedia often. You'll find that even unplanned leftovers can fit right into your menu-planning.

Refrigerator Shakedown

No matter how carefully you've planned, you're sure to have leftovers. It's not always possible to predict mealtime dropouts, fussy tastebuds or small appetites. The challenge facing all of us is planning around these budget detours to prevent waste and come out ahead. To meet this challenge, we've developed a method for using all the unplanned tidbits that inevitably accumulate in the refrigerator. We call it a "refrigerator shakedown." A refrigerator shakedown has a few rules:

1. It must be done weekly in order to ensure that the leftovers used are nutritious and appealing.

2. It's best accomplished the day you make your shopping list and plan your menus.

3. It should be done with a few basic recipes in mind—obvious ways to use the leftovers you find.

We developed the recipes in this section expressly to utilize the foods you're likely to collect during your refrigerator shakedown, especially those items that aren't left in sufficient quantity to make a second meal all by themselves. We call these recipes the "Basic Nine." Using the Basic Nine as a foundation, you can build delicious meals from the odds and ends you might otherwise just discard.

Begin your refrigerator shakedown by removing all the leftovers from the refrigerator. Then determine which can be used as is in your menu plans. Set aside the other items—foods left in small amounts and those that are too varied or just not appealing enough to be reheated and served another time. These are candidates for the Basic Nine. Depending on the other ingredients you have on hand, you can choose to make crepes, omelets, fried rice, soups, salads, quiches, sandwiches or—for a special surprise treat—a batch of Kitchen-Sink Cookies.

What if your shakedown nets you a few items that don't seem to be good material for the Basic Nine—or anything else? A half-cup of cooked oatmeal, a single egg white or a carton of starting-to-sour cottage cheese may seem destined for the garbage disposer. But before you discard anything, consult the Leftover Encyclopedia. There may be life in those leftovers yet!

Basic #1—Crepes

Crepes are one of our favorite ways of recycling small amounts of leftovers into an elegant "free" meal. You might be surprised at the potential crepes lurking in your refrigerator. Those small portions of roast beef, chicken, turkey, ham or vegetables can be combined with condensed soup, sautéed mushrooms and chopped green onions, then "gift-wrapped" in a crepe and topped with a simple sauce (see page 110) for a real VIP entree. In fact, you may choose to keep some crepes on hand in your freezer for quick company meals. We'll never tell that your specialty was created from last night's supper for mere pennies!

Basic Crepes

Crepe batter can be made up to 24 hours ahead and stored, covered, in the refrigerator.

3 eggs
Dash of salt
1-1/4 cups all-purpose flour

1-1/2 cups milk
2 tablespoons butter or margarine, melted
Filling, if desired

In a medium bowl, combine eggs and salt. Beat slightly. Gradually add flour to beaten eggs alternately with milk, beating with an electric mixer or a whisk until smooth. Beat in melted butter or margarine. Cover; refrigerate at least 1 hour or up to 24 hours. To cook crepes, use an 8- to 10-inch skillet with a nonstick finish; or brush skillet lightly with oil, margarine or butter. Heat skillet over medium-high heat. Holding heated skillet with 1 hand, pour in 2 to 3 tablespoons of batter. Quickly rotate skillet so batter covers bottom in a very thin, even layer. Return to heat; cook 45 to 60 seconds or until bottom of crepe is lightly browned. Invert skillet; let crepe drop out onto a paper towel or clean dishtowel. It's not necessary to brown second side of crepe, but if you prefer, you can flip it over for a few seconds to cook second side. If serving at once, spoon desired filling on unbrowned side of crepe; roll up and place on serving plate, seam-side down. If preparing ahead, cool crepes completely, then stack with 2 layers of wax paper between each crepe. Wrap stacked crepes in a moisture-proof freezer bag or foil, or place in an airtight plastic container. If you're freezing crepes, it's best to store them (well-wrapped) in a hard plastic container — frozen crepes are fragile and may crumble if not well protected. Refrigerate crepes 2 to 3 days or freeze up to 3 months. Thaw frozen crepes at room temperature about 1 hour before using. Or thaw and heat in a microwave oven. Makes 20 to 24 crepes.

Variation
For dessert crepes, add 2 tablespoons sugar to the batter.

Basic Meat-Filled Crepes

Vary the flavor of cream soup according to your choice of meat.

6 Basic Crepes, page 109
1 (10-3/4-oz.) can cream of mushroom soup
1-1/2 cups sliced or diced cooked beef,
    chicken, ham, pork or seafood

1/2 teaspoon Worcestershire sauce
1 tablespoon sliced green onion tops
Velouté Sauce, if desired, page 124

Prepare crepes and keep warm. In a medium saucepan, combine soup, meat or seafood, Worcestershire sauce and green onion. Cook over medium heat, stirring occasionally, until heated through. Spoon mixture into center of each warm crepe; fold crepe over to enclose. Top with Velouté Sauce, if desired. Makes 4 to 6 servings.

Egg-Surprise Crepes

The combination of cheese and eggs creates a simply delicious crepe that's a suitable entree for breakfast, brunch or supper.

12 Basic Crepes, page 109
12 eggs
1/4 cup milk
1/4 teaspoon salt
Dash of pepper
2 tablespoons butter or margarine
2 to 6 tablespoons diced vegetables
    (onions, mushrooms, green bell
    peppers, green chilies, tomatoes
    or a combination)

1/2 to 1 cup diced cooked ham, bacon,
    sausage or other meat
1 avocado, if desired, pitted, peeled, diced
Cheese Sauce, page 124
Grandma Child's Chunky Chili Sauce,
    if desired

Prepare crepes and keep warm. In medium bowl, combine eggs, milk, salt and pepper. Beat with a whisk until foamy. Set aside. In a large skillet, melt butter or margarine over medium heat. Add vegetables; sauté until firm vegetables are tender-crisp or until softer vegetables are heated through. Stir meat into egg mixture; then pour egg mixture into skillet and stir gently. Continue to cook, stirring, until eggs are almost set. Fold in avocado, if desired. Fill warm crepes; roll up or fold over to enclose filling. Top with Cheese Sauce; garnish with a little chili sauce, if desired. Serve immediately. Makes 6 to 8 servings.

Basic #2—Fried Rice

Fried rice is definitely a favorite catch-all recipe for refrigerator-shakedown day. If your shakedown produces tidbits of meat, small amounts of cooked or raw vegetables and leftover cooked rice, you have everything you need for an excellent meal. Of course, you can cook the rice fresh if you choose; just make sure to refrigerate it until cold before you use it. If the rice is used while still hot, the grains will stick together.

For more ideas for using leftover rice, see page 142.

Basic Fried Rice

Other cooked meats may be substituted for ham.

1/4 cup butter or margarine
1/4 cup chopped green onions
2 cups chilled cooked long-grain white rice
1/2 cup diced fresh mushrooms, if desired
1 cup diced raw or cooked vegetables,
   if desired

1 cup diced cooked ham
2 tablespoons soy sauce
1 egg, slightly beaten

In a large skillet, melt butter or margarine. Add green onions and rice; then stir in mushrooms and diced vegetables, if desired. Sauté about 5 minutes or until vegetables are soft. Add ham, soy sauce and egg. Stir constantly until egg is set but still moist. Makes 4 to 6 servings.

Basic #3—Omelets

Eggs and egg dishes are an appropriate choice for any meal and offer a treasure of balanced nutrients for a very nominal price. Omelets make perfect catch-alls for an unlimited variety of meats, seafood, cheese and vegetables. Even the smallest amount of these foods can be creatively seasoned or combined with other ingredients and folded into an omelet, stretching the budget and creating several bonus meals a month. To complement your omelets and add variety to your menus, take the time to master several special sauce recipes (see pages 124 and 125).

Since omelets require so little time to make, be sure to have your serving dishes and accompaniments ready and your diners close at hand before you begin to cook.

Basic French Omelet

This is a family favorite. Try topping it with chili sauce, Cheese Sauce, page 124, or sour cream.

Omelet fillings, suggestions on opposite page
2 or 3 eggs
1 tablespoon water

Salt and pepper to taste
1 to 2 tablespoons butter or margarine

Prepare your choice of filling; set aside. In a small bowl, beat eggs, water, salt and pepper until blended. In a medium skillet, melt butter or margarine over medium-high heat. As butter or margarine melts, tilt skillet in all directions to coat bottom and side thoroughly. When butter or margarine is just beginning to brown, pour in egg mixture. As soon as underside is set, quickly lift edges with a spatula, letting uncooked eggs flow underneath. Don't lift and stir vigorously or you'll end up with scrambled eggs. Cook until eggs are partially set on top, but still very soft and slightly runny in center. Spread filling over half of omelet; then use a spatula or pancake turner to carefully fold omelet in half. Cook a few seconds to warm filling; slide cooked omelet onto a serving plate. Makes 1 serving.

Suggested Fillings for Basic French Omelet:

Filling #1:
1/4 cup shredded Cheddar cheese (1 oz.)
3 bacon slices, crisp-cooked, crumbled

2 tablespoons chopped avocado

Filling #2:
1/4 cup finely chopped cooked ham
1 tablespoon snipped chives or green onion
1/4 cup chopped tomato

3 tablespoons grated cheese of your choice
3 medium fresh mushrooms, sliced

Filling #3:
1/4 cup finely chopped cooked ham
2 tablespoons chopped onion

2 tablespoons chopped green bell pepper

Variations
Any combination of meats or vegetables can be used as desired or available.

Tip
Sauces often add the gourmet touch to omelets or crepes. For some of our favorites, turn to pages 124 and 125.

How to Make Basic French Omelet

1/As soon as egg hits pan it begins to set. Cook until eggs are partially set on top, but still very soft and slightly runny in center.

2/Spread filling over half of omelet. Use a spatula or pancake turner, carefully fold unfilled omelet in half over filling.

Basic #4—Soup

Soup makes a satisfying and healthy meal, and you can have it for just pennies if you make use of leftovers. Don't throw away any bones from your roasts; there's plenty of flavor and nutrition held inside, waiting to be simmered into a flavorful broth. (Beef and pork bones should be cracked before cooking, to release more nutrients and flavor.) Freeze bones from several meals until you have enough to make a rich stock—usually 1-1/2 to 2 pounds for 1 quart of stock. Chicken necks, wings and backs, plus the scraps left after skinning and boning chicken breasts, can also be saved in the freezer. And don't forget those small portions of vegetables—a spoonful of peas here, a half-cup of carrots there. Set aside a container for them in the freezer; add leftovers as they accumulate.

We have included two basic recipes: Shakedown Soup Stock, made from either chicken or beef bones and used for making Homemade Vegetable Soup; and Encore Cream of Vegetable Soup, using leftover cooked vegetables. These are foundation recipes that you can build on to make dozens of different soups. Add all the bits and pieces of leftover meats and vegetables you find in your refrigerator shakedown; use up the "tag ends" you've stored in your freezer. The list of combinations ends only where your imagination does.

Shakedown Soup Stock

This stock may be refrigerated up to 2 days or frozen up to 4 months.

3 to 4 lbs. chicken backs, wings or necks; or 4 to 5 lbs. meaty beef bones, cracked or cut in 2- to 3-inch pieces
10 cups cold water
4 chicken or beef bouillon cubes
2 or 3 celery stalks with leaves, cut in pieces
1 medium onion, cut in quarters
1/2 teaspoon pepper
2 carrots, scrubbed, cut in large chunks
1 bay leaf
5 fresh parsley sprigs, if desired

Place chicken or beef parts or bones in a large pot. Add cold water. Bring to a boil; add bouillon cubes, celery, onion, pepper, carrots, bay leaf and parsley, if desired. Reduce heat. Cover; simmer 1 hour. Strain broth, discarding vegetables and bones. Any large pieces of meat may be reserved for making soup. Skim and discard any excess fat from broth. Use right away for making soup, or cover and refrigerate up to 2 days. Or, to freeze, pour into freezer containers, leaving 1 inch headspace. Attach lids tightly; freeze up to 4 months. Makes 3 quarts.

Homemade Vegetable Soup

The perfect winter supper to serve with crusty French bread.

**2 qts. Shakedown Soup Stock made with
chicken parts, opposite page, or 2 qts.
purchased chicken broth**
**2 cups sliced raw carrots or
leftover cooked carrots**
2 cups diced celery

1 cup diced onions
1/2 teaspoon dried leaf thyme, crushed
2 cups cooked meat and/or vegetables
**1 cup uncooked egg noodles or
    1/3 cup uncooked long-grain white rice**

In a large pot, combine stock or broth, carrots, celery, onions and thyme. Bring to a boil; reduce heat. Cover; simmer until vegetables are tender. Add cooked meat and/or vegetables and noodles or rice. Return to a boil. Cover and cook until noodles or rice are tender—7 to 10 minutes for noodles, about 20 minutes for rice. Makes 6 to 8 servings.

Variation
Beefy Vegetable Soup: Use beef broth in place of the chicken broth. Add 1 (16-oz.) can crushed stewed tomatoes.

Encore Cream of Vegetable Soup

Just about any vegetable can be pureed and used in this soup.

1 cup cooked vegetables
3 tablespoons butter or margarine
3 tablespoons all-purpose flour

**2 to 3 cups milk, chicken broth or
    a combination**
Salt and pepper to taste

Puree vegetables in a blender or a food processor fitted with a metal blade. Set aside. In a large saucepan, melt butter or margarine over low heat. Stir in flour until blended; cook, stirring, about 1 minute. Gradually add 2 cups milk or broth, stirring with a whisk until smooth. Increase heat to medium; cook until mixture thickens and begins to boil. Stir in pureed vegetables; heat thoroughly. If soup is too thick, add more milk or broth. Season with salt and pepper. Makes 4 servings.

Variation
Additional spices and herbs can be added to taste, depending on the vegetables used.

Basic #5—Salads/Dressings

Always include a variety of salad greens on your weekly shopping list. Various kinds of lettuce and other greens, such as spinach and Savoy cabbage, provide the framework for a salad bar, one of our favorite Basic Nine catch-alls. Much of what you find in your refrigerator shakedown will combine happily with greens for a make-your-own chef's salad. Use leftover cooked meat, hard-cooked eggs, cheese and raw and/or cooked vegetables. Fruits can be used, too—don't be afraid to include such foods as mandarin oranges, pineapple, apples and raisins in your selection. To give cooked vegetables added appeal, you may want to marinate them before serving. Provide a crisp topping or two, such as toasted almonds or other nuts or toasted, seasoned stale bread cubes. To pull the salad together, be sure to offer a choice of superb salad dressings. You'll find five of our favorites on pages 116 to 118.

Green salads aren't the only salads that readily accommodate leftovers; macaroni, rice and potato salads are just as agreeable. And don't forget gelatin salads. They provide a good use for leftover fruit and fruit juices; you can even puree overripe bananas and use them for part of the liquid required.

Avocado Supreme Dressing

This dressing is better if it mellows in the refrigerator for at least a day before serving.

1 large avocado, pitted, peeled, cut in chunks
1 tablespoon lemon juice
1/2 cup mayonnaise
3/4 cup dairy sour cream
2 tablespoons minced onion

1 teaspoon honey
1 garlic clove, minced
1/4 teaspoon salt
Dash of pepper

In a blender or a food processor fitted with a metal blade, combine avocado and lemon juice. Process until smooth. Add mayonnaise, sour cream, onion, honey, garlic, salt and pepper. Process until very well-blended. Cover; refrigerate up to 2 days. Makes about 2 cups.

Roquefort Dressing

Creamy, tangy Roquefort dressing is especially good served on crisp salad greens.

3/4 cup dairy sour cream
1/4 cup vegetable oil
1/4 cup evaporated milk
1 tablespoon white vinegar

1/4 teaspoon garlic powder
1/2 teaspoon salt
1/2 cup crumbled Roquefort cheese (2 oz.)

In a small bowl, stir together sour cream, oil, evaporated milk, vinegar, garlic powder and salt until well blended. Stir in cheese. Cover; refrigerate until chilled or up to 2 weeks. Makes about 1-1/2 cups.

Avocado Supreme Dressing; Roquefort Dressing; Foundation Salad Dressing, page 118; Thousand Island Supreme Dressing, page 118; Special Cashew Dressing, page 118.

Foundation Salad Dressing   *Photo on page 117.*

The framework that binds potato salads, coleslaw and macaroni salads together. You can use any type of vinegar you prefer.

1/2 cup water	3 eggs, beaten
1/2 cup vinegar	3/4 cup salad dressing or mayonnaise
1/2 cup sugar	1/2 pint whipping cream (1 cup), whipped
1 teaspoon salt	1 tablespoon sweet pickle relish,
1 teaspoon prepared mustard	if desired
1 tablespoon all-purpose flour	

In a medium saucepan, bring water, vinegar and sugar to a boil, stirring constantly until sugar is dissolved. Remove from heat; cool. Stir in salt, mustard, flour and eggs. Cook over medium heat, stirring constantly, until mixture thickens. Remove from heat; cool completely. When mixture is cool, stir in salad dressing or mayonnaise, whipped cream and pickle relish, if desired. Cover; refrigerate up to 1 week. Makes about 2 cups.

Variation
Substitute 4 egg yolks (1/3 cup) for the 3 eggs.

Thousand Island Supreme Dressing

Photo on page 117.

This is the dressing of choice at our house. The recipe was passed down from Grandma!

4 hard-cooked eggs, grated	1/4 teaspoon dry mustard
1 cup mayonnaise	2 green onions, finely chopped
1/4 cup ketchup	Salt and pepper to taste
1/4 cup sweet pickle relish	

In a small bowl, combine eggs, mayonnaise, ketchup, relish, mustard and green onions. Blend well; season with salt and pepper. Cover; refrigerate several hours or up to 1 week. Makes about 2 cups.

Special Cashew Dressing   *Photo on page 117.*

This sweet-tart dressing makes any tossed green salad special.

1/2 cup vegetable oil	2 tablespoons fresh lemon juice
1/3 cup roasted, salted cashews	1 teaspoon dried dill weed
1/4 cup water	1 teaspoon soy sauce
3 tablespoons honey	1 or 2 garlic cloves, minced

Combine all ingredients in a blender or a food processor fitted with a metal blade. Process until smooth and creamy. Cover; refrigerate up to 2 weeks. Makes about 1-1/4 cups.

Basic #6—Quiches

Your leftovers can have an elegant return engagement if you use them in a quiche. Quiche Lorraine, made with bacon, Swiss cheese and onions in a custard base, is the traditional quiche—but don't hesitate to create your own combinations based on the results of your refrigerator shakedown. For example, try substituting cubed cooked ham, chicken, sausage, shrimp or crabmeat for the bacon. Or try a vegetarian quiche filled with fresh vegetables such as spinach, zucchini, tomatoes, bell peppers, green onions and mushrooms. Vary the cheese in the custard base, too. We enjoy Swiss, Gruyère, Parmesan and Jack.

In addition to our Traditional Quiche, we include a quick-to-fix Lazy Quiche that makes its own crust as it bakes. Either is a delightful choice for a weekend brunch or a change-of-pace dinner for family and friends. And if you'd like to serve quiche as an hors d'oeuvre, and perhaps use up some leftover breakfast bacon at the same time, try the Appetizer Quichettes on page 128.

Traditional Quiche

Be as creative as you wish with this favorite supper or brunch dish.

1 (9-inch) unbaked pastry shell,
   page 53
1-1/2 cups shredded Swiss or
   Monterey Jack cheese (6 oz.)
1/2 to 1 cup diced cooked ham, bacon,
   sausage, chicken or seafood
Bits of cooked vegetables, if desired

3 eggs
1/2 teaspoon salt
1-1/2 cups half and half, whipping cream or
   milk
Paprika, if desired
Fresh parsley sprig, if desired

Preheat oven to 450F (230C). Bake pastry shell 5 minutes. Cool on a rack. Reduce oven temperature to 375F (190C). Sprinkle 3/4 cup cheese in cooled pastry shell. Top with diced meat or seafood and vegetables, if desired. In a small bowl, combine eggs, salt and half and half, cream or milk. Beat until blended, but not frothy. Pour egg mixture into pastry shell. Sprinkle with remaining 3/4 cup cheese. Bake 35 minutes or until a knife inserted in center comes out clean. Let stand 10 minutes before serving. Garnish with paprika and parsley, if desired. Makes 6 servings.

Lazy Quiche

A busy-day favorite.

1 cup diced cooked bacon, ham,
   sausage, chicken or seafood
1 cup shredded Monterey Jack cheese (4 oz.)
1 tablespoon butter or margarine
1 small onion, chopped

1-1/2 cups milk
1/2 cup biscuit mix
3 eggs
1/4 teaspoon salt

Preheat oven to 375F (190C). Lightly butter a 9-inch pie plate. Sprinkle meat or seafood and cheese in buttered pie plate. In a small skillet, melt butter or margarine over low heat. Add onion; sauté until tender, but not browned. Sprinkle onion over cheese. In a blender, combine milk, biscuit mix, eggs and salt. Process until blended. Pour over mixture in pie plate. Bake 35 to 40 minutes or until a knife inserted in center comes out clean. Let stand 5 minutes before serving. Makes 6 servings.

Basic #7—Cookies

Your first reaction to these cookies is uck—how could anyone eat cookies made from leftovers—especially tossed green salad, meat loaf, spaghetti or stew. Skeptics soon were won over with their first bite of these moist, spicy chocolate cookies. They come back for seconds. When using vinaigrette-laced tossed salad, be sure to drain out as much dressing as possible. You may wish to avoid very strong flavors or high spiced foods such as chili or fish. The texture of the leftover puree should have the consistency of thick whipped cream.

How to Make Kitchen-Sink Cookies

1/In a food processor fitted with a metal blade, puree your choice of leftovers, see list, opposite, to make 1-1/2 cups.

2/Cool cookies completely, then frost and decorate.

Kitchen-Sink Cookies

"Everything but the kitchen sink" can go into these delicious cookies.

3/4 cup butter or margarine,
  room temperature
1/2 cup granulated sugar
1/2 cup packed brown sugar
2 eggs
1 teaspoon vanilla extract
2 cups all-purpose flour
1/2 teaspoon salt
1-1/2 teaspoons baking powder
1 teaspoon ground cinnamon

1/4 cup sifted unsweetened cocoa powder
1-1/2 cups pureed leftovers, see below
3/4 cup chopped nuts
3/4 cup semisweet or milk chocolate pieces
3/4 cup raisins, if desired
3/4 cup flaked coconut, if desired
Vanilla Buttercream Icing, see below,
  if desired
Pecan or walnut halves

Vanilla Buttercream Icing:
1/2 cup butter or margarine,
  room temperature
2 cups sifted powdered sugar

1 teaspoon vanilla extract
Pinch of salt
About 2 teaspoons milk

Preheat oven to 350F (175C). Grease baking sheets. In a large bowl, combine butter or margarine, sugars, eggs and vanilla. Beat until fluffy. Beat in flour, salt, baking powder, cinnamon and cocoa powder. Add leftovers; beat well. Stir in nuts, chocolate pieces and raisins and coconut, if desired. Mix well. Drop dough by teaspoonfuls 1-1/2 inches apart on greased baking sheets. Bake 10 to 12 minutes or until set. Remove from baking sheets; transfer to racks to cool. Prepare frosting, if desired. Frost cooled cookies. Top each frosted cookie with a nut half. Makes about 48 cookies.

Suggested leftovers:
Cooked cereal, stew, cooked vegetables, leftover tossed green salad, canned or fresh fruit, cooked macaroni or other pasta, cottage cheese, leftover pancakes, waffles or muffins. You may prefer to avoid strong-flavored foods such as cauliflower and broccoli. Puree with suggested liquid below to make 1-1/2 cups. Consistency of puree should be like thick whipped cream.

Suggested liquids for pureeing (if necessary):
Water, fruit juice, milk, chocolate milk.

Vanilla Buttercream Icing:
In a medium bowl, beat butter or margarine, powdered sugar, vanilla, salt and milk until fluffy. Makes about 2 cups.

Variation
Kitchen-Sink Bar Cookies: Grease a 13'' x 9'' baking pan. Spread cookie dough in pan; Bake 30 to 40 minutes. Do not overbake; cookies should be moist. Cool in pan on a rack. Frost, if desired. Cut into bars (about 2-1/4'' x 1''). Makes 48 cookies.

Basic #8—Make-a-Sandwich

This easy-to-read Make-a-Sandwich chart provides suggestions for a variety of delicious sandwiches. You choose the kind of sandwich according to what you've collected during your refrigerator shakedown.

LEFTOVER ITEM	BREAD	SPREAD	ADDITIONAL INGREDIENTS
ROAST BEEF			
Sliced	Rye or whole-wheat	Butter or margarine with dash of lemon juice and mustard	Prepared horseradish, onion slices, lettuce leaf or sauerkraut
	Pita or whole-wheat	Butter or margarine mustard, mayonnaise	Sautéed onion slices, mushrooms (HEAT sandwich)
Bits and pieces, ground	White or whole-wheat	Butter or margarine	Mix with chopped sweet pickles or relish, mayonnaise and/or sour cream
PORK			
Sliced	White or whole-wheat	Butter or margarine	Top with gravy; serve open-faced (HEAT meat and gravy)
Shredded	French roll	Butter or margarine	Barbecue sauce (HEAT sandwich)
TURKEY			
Sliced	Pumpernickel	Butter or margarine	Egg salad, dash of curry powder, lettuce
	French	Butter or mayonnaise	Cranberry sauce, leftover stuffing
	Sourdough French, toasted	Butter or margarine	Top with jack cheese and green chilies (HEAT or BROIL sandwich)
	rye	Thousand Island dressing	Tomato slices, hard-cooked egg slices, Swiss cheese
	Kaiser roll	Blue cheese dressing	Shredded lettuce, tomato slices
	White or whole-wheat toast	Butter or margarine	Leftover stuffing, cranberry sauce, gravy (HEAT meat, stuffing and gravy)
CHICKEN			
Sliced	White or whole-wheat	Butter or margarine; lemon juice and ground oregano or thyme	Lettuce, tomato slices
	Whole-wheat hard roll	Cream cheese Butter or margarine	Walnuts, alfalfa sprouts, avocado slices, barbecue sauce (HEAT sandwich)
Chopped or ground	White or whole-wheat	Butter or margarine	Mix with diced celery, mayonnaise, seasoned salt, chopped hard-cooked eggs, sliced stuffed or black olives

LEFTOVER ITEM	BREAD	SPREAD	ADDITIONAL INGREDIENTS
HAM			
Sliced	Rye or pumpernickel	Butter or margarine, tangy sweet mustard and/or mayonnaise	Swiss or Cheddar cheese, green chilies (GRILL sandwich)
	Whole-wheat bun	Guacamole	Top with alfalfa sprouts, tomato slices, jack cheese; serve open-faced (BROIL sandwich)
Ground	White or whole-wheat	Butter or margarine	Mix with celery, pickle relish, prepared horseradish, mayonnaise
Diced	Hollowed-out hard roll		Mix with grated cheese, minced onion, chopped olives, green chilies, tomato juice, lemon juice; fill roll (WRAP and HEAT sandwich)
	Pumpernickel	Butter or margarine	Mix with shredded Swiss cheese, chopped tomato and green onion, mayonnaise (HEAT sandwich)
	Large hard roll	Butter or margarine	Mix with scrambled egg, chopped onion, chopped green bell pepper, seasoning (HEAT sandwich)
EGGS			
Hard-cooked	White, whole-wheat or rye toast	Butter or margarine with dash of lemon juice, paprika	Mix with mayonnaise, salt, pepper, dash of dry mustard; if desired, add chopped sweet pickle, green onion, sliced stuffed olives
Deviled	English muffin	Butter or margarine	Place eggs on muffin halves; top with White sauce and serve open-faced
CHEESE			
Diced	White or whole-wheat	Butter or margarine	Mix with mayonnaise plus any of the following: chopped chicken, chopped sweet pickles, hard-cooked eggs, olives, tuna or ham
MEATBALLS			
In Sauce	French roll	Butter or margarine	Sautéed onions and green bell peppers, grated Parmesan cheese (HEAT sandwich)
MEAT LOAF	Sourdough French	Butter or margarine, ketchup	Lettuce

> ## Basic #9—Sauces
> A carefully chosen sauce can turn an otherwise ordinary meal into a culinary classic. By mastering these few basic sauces, you'll reinforce your reputation as a great cook.

Basic White Sauce

This makes a medium-thick white sauce. For a thicker sauce, increase butter or margarine and flour by 1 tablespoon each. For a thinner sauce, decrease butter or margarine and flour by 1 tablespoon each.

2 tablespoons butter or margarine
2 tablespoons all-purpose flour
1 cup milk, chicken broth,
   beef broth or a combination

Salt and pepper to taste

In a small saucepan, melt butter or margarine over low heat. Stir in flour until blended. Cook, stirring constantly, about 1 minute. Slowly add milk or broth, stirring with a whisk until smooth. Continue to cook and stir until bubbly and thickened. Season with salt and pepper. Makes 1 cup.

Variations
Velouté Sauce: Use chicken broth or fish stock for the liquid.
Mornay Sauce: Use 1/2 cup chicken broth and 1/2 cup milk for the liquid. After sauce has thickened, add 2 tablespoons shredded Swiss cheese and 2 tablespoons grated Parmesan cheese; stir until cheese is melted.
Cheese Sauce: Use milk for the liquid; add 1/2 teaspoon dry mustard with the flour. After sauce has thickened, add 1/2 to 1 cup shredded Cheddar, Swiss or Monterey Jack cheese (2 to 4 oz.). Stir until cheese is melted.

Serving suggestions:
Basic White Sauce: Use for creaming vegetables and fish and as a binder for casseroles and crepe fillings. Use as the base for soups and many other sauces.
Velouté Sauce: Serve as an accompaniment to chicken, veal, fish and vegetables.
Mornay Sauce: Serve as an accompaniment to fish, eggs and vegetables.
Cheese Sauce: Serve as an accompaniment to vegetables and egg dishes.

Sweet Butter Sauce

Scrumptious served over apple and mincemeat pies, steamed puddings, cakes and many other desserts.

1/2 cup butter
1 cup sugar
1/2 pint whipping cream (1 cup) or
   1 cup evaporated milk

Dash of ground nutmeg

Combine butter, sugar and cream or evaporated milk in a small saucepan. Cook, stirring, over medium heat 3 to 5 minutes or until butter is melted and sugar is dissolved. Do not boil. Remove from heat; add nutmeg. Serve warm. Makes about 1-1/4 cups.

Sauce Béarnaise

This sauce should be served warm rather than hot.

3 tablespoons white-wine vinegar
1 tablespoon dried leaf tarragon, crushed
3 tablespoons finely chopped green onions
1/4 teaspoon salt

Dash of freshly ground pepper
3 egg yolks (1/4 cup), beaten
3/4 cup butter, melted, cooled
1/2 cup half and half

In a heavy saucepan, combine vinegar, tarragon, green onions, salt and pepper. Bring to a boil over medium heat; boil until almost all liquid has evaporated. Remove from heat; add egg yolks. Return pan to heat; stir with a whisk until sauce has thickened to the consistency of mayonnaise. Slowly pour melted, cooled butter into sauce in a thin stream. Stir in half and half. Serve immediately. Makes about 1-1/4 cups.

Serving suggestions:
Serve as an accompaniment to most broiled red meats, especially beef tenderloin. Sauce Béarnaise is also good with fish and eggs.

Make-Ahead Hollandaise Sauce

The secret to good hollandaise is to start with the ingredients at room temperature.

1/2 cup butter, melted, cooled to
   room temperature
3 egg yolks (1/4 cup), beaten

1 tablespoon fresh lemon juice
3 tablespoons half and half
Salt and red (cayenne) pepper to taste

About 1 hour before serving, combine butter, egg yolks, lemon juice and half and half in a heavy saucepan. Beat with a whisk just until mixed. Let stand at room temperature until 3 minutes before serving. Then cook over medium heat, stirring constantly, until thickened. Season with salt and red pepper; serve immediately. Makes 1 cup.

Variation
Mousseline Sauce: Just before serving, stir in 1/2 cup whipping cream, whipped.

Serving suggestions
Make-Ahead Hollandaise Sauce: Serve as an accompaniment to most vegetable, egg and meat dishes.
Mousseline Sauce: Serve as an accompaniment to vegetables and seafood dishes.

Leftover Encyclopedia

Don't throw it out! That last tablespoon of jam or relish and even the brine from pickles can be put to good use. The same holds true for beef bones, leftover oatmeal, and many other items that most of us toss out as garbage. For example, the vitamin-rich potato peels usually consigned to the trash are easily made into our Potato Skin Snacks for a simple after-school treat—a good way to save money and add nutrition to your family's diet at the same time.

In this encyclopedia, you'll find suggestions for using a number of things, from apple peels to leftover whipped cream. Be sure to check our Revitalizing Tips, too; you can easily salvage that limp celery or rock-hard brown sugar. And before you ever throw out any edible food, decide whether it can be used in one of our Basic Nine recipes. Kitchen-Sink Cookies, page 121, are guaranteed to accommodate any item and turn it into a delicious drop or bar cookie.

Apple peels: Collect in your freezer; use to make apple jelly. There's a recipe on most packages of pectin.

Bacon: See opposite page.

Bacon grease: Save in a container; use in breads for better flavor.

Bones from meat; chicken backs, wings and necks: Collect in your freezer. Use ham bones to flavor a pot of beans or soup. Pork bones add flavor to spaghetti sauce and other Italian sauces; (see Spaghetti Sauce Supreme, page 45). Beef bones and chicken parts can be used to make delicious broths for soups—Shakedown Soup Stock, page 114, for example.

Bread, buns, toast, crusts: See page 129.

Butter or margarine wrappers: Store in a bag in your refrigerator; use to grease baking pans or skillets or butter the top of freshly baked breads.

Buttermilk or soured milk: See page 130.

Cakes, cookies, muffins and sweet breads that have dried out: Crumble to make crumbs. Keep in a covered jar in your freezer; add other crumbs as they accumulate. Use as a topping for ice cream or puddings or as a garnish for other desserts.

Cereals (cooked Cream of Wheat, oatmeal): Add to doughs when making breads. Or add a beaten egg to leftover mush; spoon mixture into a loaf pan, cover and refrigerate. For breakfast the next day, unmold the chilled mush; slice. Fry slices on both sides in melted butter or margarine. Serve with syrup or jam.

Citrus peels (lemon, orange): Pare off colored part; dry out. Grate by hand or process in a blender or a food processor fitted with a metal blade. Keep in covered containers in the freezer; use in recipes calling for grated lemon or orange peel.

Cottage cheese: See page 133.

Cream, whipped: A little bit of leftover whipped cream can be frozen in dollops on a sheet of wax paper. When the mounds of cream are frozen solid, store them in a covered container in the freezer until needed. Use to top ice cream, pudding, gelatin and other desserts.

Egg yolks, egg whites, hard-cooked eggs: See pages 134 through 140.

Juices from canned or cooked fruits and vegetables: Keep separate containers in your freezer, one for fruit juices and one for most vegetable juices. Store strong-flavored vegetable juices, such as broccoli or asparagus cooking water, in a third container; reserve for recipes in which the strong flavor will be unnoticeable or unobjectionable.

Use fruit juices for punch bases, in gelatin salads or to make "ice" cubes for lemonade or carbonated beverages. Fruit juices make a nice dessert sauce, too. Place 1 cup of fruit juices in a small pan; add 1 tablespoon lemon juice and 1 tablespoon cornstarch. Cook until thickened, stirring constantly. Remove from heat; add 1 tablespoon butter or margarine. This sauce is especially good over warm gingerbread; it's tasty with cakes, puddings, ice cream and other desserts as well. For a fruit-salad dressing, cool sauce completely, then fold it into whipped cream.

Vegetable cooking water and the liquid from canned vegetables are rich in vitamins and minerals and should always be saved. Use this nutrition-packed liquid in mashed potatoes and as part of the liquid in soups, gravies and sauces. Potato cooking water is also good in yeast breads—it actually speeds rising!

Miscellaneous bottled foods (ideas for using the last bit):

Jam jar: Fill with milk and crushed ice, shake up, and presto! A fruit-flavored drink for the little ones.

Ketchup bottle: To make a French salad dressing, add

vinegar, vegetable oil, mixed herbs, salt and a few drops of hot-pepper sauce; shake to blend.

Mayonnaise jar: Add vinegar, vegetable oil and crumbled blue cheese for a tasty salad dressing.

Mustard jar: Add a little vegetable oil and vinegar and shake to blend. Use for a different salad dressing or as a marinade for vegetables.

Relish jar: Add some mayonnaise and a dash of hot-pepper sauce for a quick, inexpensive tartar sauce.

Pancakes, waffles, French toast: We can buy all these items frozen, packaged as convenience foods. Why not package your leftovers in bags or containers in the freezer? Just pop one in the toaster for a quick, no-fuss breakfast.

Pickle juices: These can be used as marinades and in salad dressings and potato salads. Or add about 1/4 cup to stews and pot roasts to tenderize the meat.

When you've eaten a jar of sweet pickles and only the juice remains, drain a can of beets and add it to the pickle jar. Refrigerate a few days and you've created your own pickled beets.

Potato skins, cooked potatoes: Collect skins in a container in the freezer to toss with melted butter, garlic salt and pepper. Bake at 475F (245C) until crisp. Use cooked potatoes in Norwegian Lefse, page 140, and other recipes.

Puddings: Spoon small amounts of leftover pudding into small paper cups. Insert a Popsicle stick or plastic spoon in the center of each. Freeze to make your own pudding pops.

Tomato paste: When a recipe calls for only part of a can of tomato paste, freeze the remainder in dollops on wax paper. When the mounds are frozen solid, store them in a covered container in the freezer until needed for another recipe.

Tossed salad: It's difficult to estimate the exact amount of tossed green salad you'll need. If there's any leftover, and there usually is, it often gets pitched out because it wilts and seems unusable. But in fact, wilted salad has its uses. It can be pureed in the blender, heated and served as soup. Or freeze the puree to use in making soup at your convenience.

Water used to boil eggs: Cool water; use it to water your houseplants. They'll really flourish.

REVITALIZING TIPS

Some items seem destined for the trash can because of the state they're in. Obviously, there's nothing you can do for a rotten onion or bread that's blue with mold. But other foods — such as hardened brown sugar, limp greens, or cornflakes that have lost their crunch — can be restored to usable condition quite easily.

To soften brown sugar: Place in an airtight container along with a slice of fresh bread or a wedge of apple. Cover tightly. Within a day or two, your brown sugar will be as soft as when it was purchased.

To re-crisp celery, lettuce and other salad greens: Rinse in hot water, then in ice water with a little vinegar added. Or put the wilted vegetables in a pan of cold water; add a few slices of raw potato. Let soak 1 hour or until crisp. Vegetables will crisp more quickly if you place the pan in the refrigerator.

To liquefy crystallized honey: Slowly heat, stirring, but do not boil. Or set the jar of honey in a pan full of very hot water; let stand, stirring occasionally, until liquefied.

To reserve and reheat baked potatoes: Dip in hot water. Bake in a 350F (175C) oven, 20 minutes.

To freshen and re-crisp stale cereal and crackers: Spread on a baking sheet; heat in a preheated 200F (95C) oven, about 5 minutes.

Bacon

2 bacon slices = 1 to 2 tablespoons crisp-cooked, crumbled bacon

Suggestions for use: Use in bacon and tomato sandwiches and in salads; use as a garnish for soups and vegetables; use bacon grease in place of vegetable oil in pancakes, breads and muffins.

Recipes included:
Appetizer Quichettes, page 128
Basic Nine recipes (Chapter 5):
   Crepes, page 109
   Fried Rice, page 111
   Make-a-Sandwich, page 122
   Omelets, page 112
   Quiches, page 119

How to Make Appetizer Quichettes

1/Divide cheese, sautéed onion and bacon among pastry lined tart or mini muffin pans. Pour egg mixture evenly into tarts; completely cover ingredients.

2/Bake as directed. Let stand 5 minutes before removing from pans. Serve warm or at room temperature. Cover and refrigerate if not used within 2 hours. Tarts may be frozen up to 3 month.

Appetizer Quichettes

These freeze well after baking and can be reheated without thawing.

Basic Tart Pastry, see below
**2/3 cup finely shredded Swiss cheese
   (2-2/3 oz.)**
1 tablespoon butter or margarine
1 small onion, finely chopped
4 to 6 bacon slices, crisp-cooked, crumbled
2 eggs, slightly beaten

1 cup milk
1/4 teaspoon salt
Dash of pepper
**1/8 teaspoon ground nutmeg or
   1/4 teaspoon dry mustard**

Basic Tart Pastry:
**1/2 cup butter or margarine,
   room temperature**
**1 (3-oz.) pkg. cream cheese,
   room temperature**

1 cup all-purpose flour

Prepare Basic Tart Pastry; opposite page. Press each ball of pastry over bottom and up side of a 1-1/2- to 2-inch mini-muffin cups. Preheat oven to 450F (230C). Divide cheese evenly among pastry-lined pans, putting about 3/4 teaspoon in bottom of each. In a small skillet, melt butter or margarine. Add onion; sauté 2 to 3 minutes or until tender but not browned. Divide onion evenly among tarts, then top evenly with bacon. In a 2-cup measuring cup, beat eggs, milk, salt, pepper and nutmeg or mustard. Pour egg mixture evenly into tarts. Bake 10 minutes. Reduce oven temperature to 350F (175C) and continue to bake 10 more minutes. Let stand 5 minutes before serving. If preparing ahead; cool. Package airtight; freeze up to 3 months. To reheat, bake frozen quichettes in a 450F (230C) oven, 10 minutes or until heated through. Makes 40 quichettes.

Recipe directions continued on next page.

Basic Tart Pastry:
In a medium bowl, beat butter or margarine and cream cheese until smooth. Add flour; knead until you can form dough into a ball. Divide dough into 40 equal portions; shape each into a ball.

Variation
Substitute diced cooked ham, small cooked shrimp, crabmeat or other meat or vegetables for the bacon.

Breads, buns, toast, crusts

Stale bread, leftover toast and bread crusts have a surprising number of uses. Turn them into croutons, stuffing or bread pudding, or use them in any of the other ways suggested below.

If you decide to turn your stale bread into bread crumbs, plan on getting about 1/4 to 1/3 cup crumbs from each dry slice, about 3/4 to 1 cup from each softer slice.

Suggestions for use: Use in puddings, stratas, stuffings, French toast, croutons; use as a meatball or meat loaf extender; cube or crumble as a topping for casseroles; cube for dippers in cheese fondue; toast for milk toast; process in a blender or a food processor fitted with a metal blade to make bread crumbs.

Recipes included:
Caramel-Topped Bread Pudding, page 93
Chicken Kiev, page 43
Crisp Toast Cups, page 130
Julie's Ham Loaves, page 60
Make-Ahead Meat Loaf, page 49
No-Fail Cheese Soufflé, page 95
Poulet D'Artichoke, page 73
Super Stuffing, below

Super Stuffing

Your family may prefer this savory stuffing to potatoes as a side dish.

4 cups dry 1/2-inch bread cubes (including crusts)	**1/2 teaspoon salt**
1/4 cup butter or margarine	**1/4 teaspoon pepper**
1 medium onion, finely chopped	**3/4 teaspoon ground sage**
2 celery stalks with leaves, finely chopped	**1 egg, beaten**
	1/2 cup chicken broth, or more if desired

Put bread cubes in a large bowl. Preheat oven to 350F (175C). Butter a 1-1/2-quart casserole dish. In a medium skillet, melt butter or margarine. Add onion and celery; sauté until onion is tender but not browned. Remove from heat; stir in salt, pepper, sage, egg and broth. If you prefer a moister stuffing, use more broth. Pour mixture over bread cubes. Toss to mix; spoon into buttered dish. Bake 35 to 40 minutes or until heated through. Makes about 6 servings.

Variations
Cornbread Stuffing: Substitute 3 cups crumbled cornbread for the bread cubes.
Nut Stuffing: Add 1/4 cup chopped walnuts or diced water chestnuts.
Sausage & Apple Stuffing: Add 1/2 cup cooked, crumbled sausage and 1 small apple, finely chopped.
Poultry Stuffing: Use Super Stuffing or any of the variations to stuff a 10- to 12-lb. turkey.

Crisp Toast Cups

Fill with scrambled eggs or your favorite creamed vegetables.

12 slices day-old white bread
6 tablespoons butter or margarine, melted

Preheat oven to 375F (190C). Cut crusts from bread. Carefully press trimmed bread slices into ungreased 2-1/2-inch muffin cups. Brush bread with melted butter or margarine. Bake 10 to 12 minutes or until lightly browned. Cool in pans on a rack; remove from pans. If preparing ahead, place cooled toast cups in a single layer in an airtight container. Freeze up to 3 months. Makes 12 toast cups.

Caramel-Topped Bread Pudding

When unmolded, this pudding forms its own rich sauce.

3/4 cup packed brown sugar
1/2 cup raisins
3 slices day-old white bread
2 tablespoons butter or margarine,
   room temperature
3 eggs

1 pint milk (2 cups)
1 teaspoon vanilla extract
1/4 teaspoon salt
1/2 pint whipping cream (1 cup)

Preheat oven to 350F (175C). Butter a 1-1/2-quart casserole buttered dish. Sprinkle brown sugar over bottom of dish. Sprinkle raisins over brown sugar. Spread both sides of bread slices with butter or margarine. Cut buttered bread in 1/2-inch cubes. Arrange bread cubes over raisins. In a medium bowl, beat eggs with a whisk. Add milk, vanilla and salt; mix well. Pour over bread in dish. Place dish in a shallow baking pan. Pour enough boiling water into baking pan to come 1 inch up side of dish. Bake 50 to 60 minutes or until a knife inserted near center comes out clean. Lift dish from water; let stand 10 minutes. Meanwhile, if desired, whip and sweeten cream. Loosen pudding around edge of dish with a knife. Spoon into individual bowls. Serve hot with cream or whipped cream. Makes 6 servings.

Buttermilk

Don't throw out the last cup of buttermilk in the carton—or even milk that's turned sour. Both buttermilk and soured milk can be used in a wide variety of baked goods, from waffles to fancy layer cakes. Buttermilk and soured milk are not substitutes for recipes calling for milk. Buttermilk also adds fresh, tangy flavor to dips and salad dressings.

Note: Buttermilk and soured milk are not substitutes for milk—so if a recipe calls for milk, don't use buttermilk or soured milk in its place. If you need to use up soured milk, it's best to use it in baking. Don't substitute soured milk for buttermilk in dips or dressings, where the flavor of buttermilk is important.

Suggestions for use: Use in pancakes, waffles, muffins, cakes; use buttermilk in dips and dressings.

Recipes included:
Basic Buttermilk Pancakes, opposite page
Buttermilk Waffles Supreme, opposite page
Fried Zucchini (Garlic Dip for), page 32
Overnight Basic Buttermilk Dough, page 99
   Parker House Rolls
   Crescent Rolls
   Orange Crescent Rolls
   Caramel-Pecan Rolls
   Mini-Buns
   Soft Breadsticks
   Fried Scones
Raisin-Molasses Muffins, page 98

Basic Buttermilk Pancakes

Refrigerate or freeze leftover batter in an airtight container for another day.

1 cup all-purpose flour
2 tablespoons sugar
1/2 teaspoon salt
1/2 teaspoon baking soda

1 egg
1 cup buttermilk
3 tablespoons butter or margarine, melted

Preheat an electric griddle to 375F (190C) or heat a skillet over medium heat. In a small bowl, sift together flour, sugar, salt and baking soda. In a medium bowl, beat together egg and buttermilk. Add flour mixture to buttermilk mixture, beating until smooth. Blend in melted butter or margarine. If preparing batter ahead, cover; refrigerate up to 12 hours or freeze up to 2 weeks. To cook, lightly grease hot griddle or skillet. Pour batter on griddle or skillet, using about 1/4 cup for each pancake. Cook until bottoms of pancakes are golden brown and bubbles begin to break through the surface. Turn pancakes; cook until golden brown on other side. Makes about 8 (4-inch) pancakes.

Variations
Apple Buttermilk Pancakes: Fold 1 cup chopped apples into batter.
Blueberry Buttermilk Pancakes: Stir in 1/2 cup well-drained canned blueberries or 1 cup fresh or frozen blueberries just before cooking.
Strawberry Buttermilk Pancakes: Fold 1 cup thinly sliced strawberries into batter.
Pineapple Buttermilk Pancakes: Fold 1 (8-oz.) can crushed pineapple, drained well, into batter.
Banana Buttermilk Pancakes: Fold 1 diced banana into batter.

Buttermilk Waffles Supreme   *Photo on page 132.*

If you mix up the batter tonight, you'll have a hassle-free breakfast tomorrow morning.

2 cups all-purpose flour
2 teaspoons baking powder
3/4 teaspoon baking soda
1/2 teaspoon salt

3 tablespoons sugar
4 eggs, separated
1 pint buttermilk (2 cups)
1/4 cup butter or margarine, melted

Preheat a waffle baker. In a medium bowl, sift together flour, baking powder, baking soda, salt and sugar; set aside. In a large bowl, beat egg whites until stiff; set aside. In another large bowl, beat egg yolks and buttermilk until blended. Add flour mixture to buttermilk mixture; blend well. Stir in melted butter or margarine. Fold in beaten egg whites. If preparing batter ahead, cover; refrigerate up to 12 hours. To cook, bake waffles in preheated waffle baker according to manufacturer's directions. Makes 4 (12-inch-square) waffles.

Variation
No-Fuss Buttermilk Waffles: Do not separate eggs. Beat together eggs and buttermilk; add to flour mixture. Stir in melted butter or margarine.

Cottage Cheese

What do you do with a carton of cottage cheese that's just beginning to sour? One thing you shouldn't do is throw it away. It can still be successfully used in baked goods and other recipes; see the list below. Don't toss out the last half-cup in the carton, either; try adding it to scrambled eggs or using it as a sour-cream substitute.

Suggestions for use: Use in breads or scrambled eggs; use as a low-calorie substitute for sour cream by blending in blender with 1 tablespoon milk and 1 teaspoon lemon juice for every 1 cup cottage cheese; use as a substitute for ricotta cheese in Italian recipes.

Recipes included:
Cottage-Cheese Bread, page 134
Crispy Biscuits, below
Doubly Delicious Layered Tamale Bake, page 48
Green Chili & Rice Bake, below
Mashed-Potato Delight, page 96

Green Chili & Rice Bake

A versatile recipe — it's both an excellent main dish and a tasty side dish.

3 cups cooked long-grain white rice
8 oz. cottage cheese (1 cup)
1 pint dairy sour cream (2 cups)
2 tablespoons butter or margarine

1 cup chopped onions
1 (4-oz.) can diced green chilies
2-1/2 cups shredded Cheddar cheese (10 oz.)
2 teaspoons dried parsley flakes

Preheat oven to 350F (175C). Grease a 2-quart casserole dish. In a large bowl, combine rice, cottage cheese and sour cream; set aside. In a small skillet, melt butter or margarine over medium heat. Add onions; sauté until golden, then add to rice mixture. Stir in chilies and 1-1/2 cups cheese. Spread 1/2 of mixture in greased dish. Sprinkle with 1/2 cup remaining cheese and 1 teaspoon parsley flakes. Top with remaining rice mixture, spreading evenly; sprinkle with remaining 1/2 cup cheese and remaining 1 teaspoon parsley flakes. Bake, uncovered, 30 minutes or until heated through. Makes 6 to 8 servings.

Crispy Biscuits

A great way to use cottage cheese that's starting to sour.

2-1/4 cups all-purpose flour
1 tablespoon baking powder
3/4 teaspoon baking soda
1/2 teaspoon salt
1 tablespoon sugar

1/4 cup vegetable shortening
2 tablespoons butter or margarine
2 eggs, lightly beaten
8 oz. cream-style cottage cheese (1 cup)
Melted butter or margarine

Preheat oven to 425F (220C). Lightly grease a large baking sheet. In a medium bowl, combine flour, baking powder, baking soda, salt and sugar. Using a pastry blender, cut in shortening and 2 tablespoons butter or margarine until mixture resembles cornmeal. In another bowl, beat together eggs and cottage cheese with a whisk until combined. Add egg mixture to flour mixture; toss with a fork to combine. On a lightly floured surface, knead dough 8 to 10 times to form a ball. Roll out dough to about 1/2 inch thick; cut out biscuits with a round 2-1/2-inch cutter. Place biscuits 1 inch apart on greased baking sheet. Brush with melted butter or margarine. Bake 10 to 12 minutes or until golden. Makes about 16 biscuits.

Buttermilk Waffles Supreme, page 131.

Cottage-Cheese Bread

This is our families' favorite bread. It has a nice golden crust and a wonderful soft, tender crumb.

1 cup warm water (110F, 45C)
1 tablespoon sugar
3 (1/4-oz.) pkgs. active dry yeast
   (3 tablespoons)
1/2 cup instant potato flakes
1 cup boiling water
8 oz. cottage cheese (1 cup)
1/2 teaspoon baking soda
1/2 cup sugar

1 tablespoon salt
1/4 cup vegetable oil or
   1/4 cup butter or margarine, melted
2 eggs, beaten
7 to 8 cups all-purpose flour or
   3-1/2 to 4 cups each all-purpose flour
   and whole-wheat flour
Melted butter or margarine

In a small bowl, combine warm water and 1 tablespoon sugar. Sprinkle in yeast; set aside. In a large bowl (or in large bowl of a heavy-duty mixer) combine potato flakes, boiling water, cottage cheese, baking soda, 1/2 cup sugar, salt, oil or melted butter or margarine and eggs. Beat well to mix. Cool to lukewarm (110F, 45C); stir in yeast mixture. Beating with an electric mixer, add 4 cups flour. If using a heavy-duty mixer, gradually beat in remaining 3 to 4 cups flour to make a soft, but not sticky dough. If not using a heavy-duty mixer, turn out batter onto a well-floured surface; knead in remaining flour. Knead 10 minutes or until smooth. Cover; let rise in a warm place about 1 hour or until doubled in bulk. Generously grease 3 (9'' x 5'') loaf pans or 4 (8-1/2'' x 4-1/2'') loaf pans. Punch down dough; shape into 3 or 4 loaves. Place loaves in greased pans. Let rise until slightly rounded over tops of pans. Preheat oven to 400F (205C). Bake 15 minutes; then reduce oven temperature to 350F (175C) and continue to bake 20 more minutes. Brush tops of loaves with melted butter or margarine. Remove from pans; cool on racks. Makes 3 or 4 loaves.

Eggs

The odd egg yolk or egg white may seem useless to you. But even a single yolk or white has a multitude of uses. And if you have several, you'll be equipped to make a number of recipes. Collect egg yolks in a covered container in the refrigerator, keeping them covered with cold water; they'll keep up to 3 days. Store egg whites in the refrigerator up to 2 weeks (or in the freezer up to 12 months), adding more to the container until you've accumulated enough for angel food cake or meringues.

Hard-cooked eggs have numerous uses, too; see the suggestions on page 140.

12 large egg whites = 1-1/2 cups egg whites
4 egg yolks = 1/3 cup egg yolks
12 hard-cooked eggs = 3-1/2 cups chopped eggs

Egg yolks:

Suggestions for use: Use as a thickening for puddings, sauces, custards, pie fillings and salad dressings; add to scrambled eggs; use 2 egg yolks plus 1 tablespoon water in place of 1 whole egg in baked goods; use in sponge and yellow cakes; brush on breads before baking as a glaze; poach in simmering water until hard-cooked, force through a sieve and use as a garnish for salads, soups and vegetables.

Recipes included:
Asparagus with Orange Hollandaise Sauce, page 15
Foundation Salad Dressing (variation), page 118
French Cream Pie, page 103
Lemon Cloud Pie, opposite page
Make-Ahead Hollandaise Sauce, page 125
Melt-in-Your-Mouth Butter Cookies, opposite page
Mousseline Sauce, page 125
Potato Nests, page 29
Seafood Wellington, page 92
Strawberry-Rum-Cream Cake, page 104
Sweet English Custard Sauce, page 136

Melt-in-Your-Mouth Butter Cookies

These will bring back memories of childhood days.

1 cup butter or margarine,
  room temperature
1 cup sugar
2 egg yolks
1 teaspoon lemon extract or vanilla extract

2-1/2 cups all-purpose flour
1-1/2 teaspoons baking soda
1/4 teaspoon salt
About 1 tablespoon water
Sugar

Preheat oven to 350F (175C). Grease 2 large baking sheets. In a medium bowl, cream butter or margarine and 1 cup sugar. Add egg yolks and lemon extract or vanilla. Mix well. In another medium bowl, combine flour, baking soda and salt. Stir flour mixture into creamed mixture. Stir in about 1 tablespoon water or enough to make dough hold together. Form dough into walnut-size balls. Dip each ball in sugar; place sugared-side up, 2 inches apart on greased baking sheets. Flatten balls with tines of a fork. Bake 10 to 12 minutes or until lightly browned around edges. Remove from baking sheets and cool completely on racks. Makes 36 to 42 cookies.

Variation
Do not dip balls in sugar. Instead, place balls on baking sheet, then make a deep indentation in the middle of each. Fill indentation with jam of your choice. Bake as directed.

Lemon Cloud Pie

A light, tart filling well worth the pucker!

4 egg yolks (1/3 cup)
1/2 cup granulated sugar
7 tablespoons fresh lemon juice
2 tablespoons grated lemon peel

1 pint whipping cream (2 cups)
1/2 cup sifted powdered sugar
1 teaspoon vanilla extract
1 (9-inch) baked pastry shell, page 53

In a medium bowl, beat egg yolks until light. Add granulated sugar, lemon juice and 1 tablespoon lemon peel. Pour mixture into a medium, heavy saucepan. Cook over medium-high heat 5 minutes or until mixture is very thick, stirring constantly. Remove from heat; cool. In a large bowl, beat cream until stiff peaks form. Fold in powdered sugar and vanilla. Place 1/2 of whipped cream in a medium bowl; set aside. Fold cooled egg-yolk mixture into remaining whipped cream; spoon mixture into pastry shell. Spread reserved whipped cream over filling. Sprinkle remaining 1 tablespoon lemon peel over whipped cream. Refrigerate at least 2 hours before serving. Makes 6 to 8 servings.

How to Make Sweet English Custard Sauce

1/Cook, stirring constantly, until custard thickens enough to lightly coat a metal spoon.

2/Cool, cover; refrigerate until chilled. Add lemon peel before serving, if desired. Pour over fresh fruit or cake cubes.

Sweet English Custard Sauce

This makes a delicious topping for any combination of berries; it can also be layered in parfaits.

6 egg yolks (1/2 cup)
1 pint warm milk (2 cups)
1/2 cup sugar

1 teaspoon vanilla extract
1 teaspoon finely grated lemon peel, if desired

In the top of a double boiler or in a heavy saucepan, combine egg yolks, milk and sugar. Stir with a whisk until blended. Place over simmering water (or over low direct heat, if using a saucepan). Cook, stirring constantly, until custard thickens enough to lightly coat a metal spoon. If using a saucepan, watch closely to prevent scorching. Remove from heat; stir in vanilla. Cover and refrigerate. Add lemon peel before serving, if desired. Makes about 2-1/2 cups.

Egg whites:

Suggestions for use: Use in meringues, baked Alaska, white-cake mixes, angel food cakes, soufflés, boiled icings, macaroons, frosted grape garnish; add to mashed potatoes to make them fluffier; use to glaze breads before baking; add to scrambled eggs.

Recipes included:

Secret Meringue Pie

Butter crackers are the secret to the unique flavor of this wonderful ice-cream-sundae pie.

3 egg whites (6 tablespoons),
   room temperature
1/2 teaspoon baking powder
1 cup sugar
17 round or oval butter crackers, crushed

1 cup finely chopped pecans
1 qt. vanilla ice cream
1-1/2 cups purchased chocolate sauce or
   chocolate syrup

Preheat oven to 325F (165C). Lightly butter a 9-inch pie plate. In a medium bowl, combine egg whites and baking powder. Beat with an electric mixer until foamy. Gradually add sugar; continue to beat until stiff. Fold in crushed crackers and pecans. Spread mixture over bottom and up side of buttered pie plate, building up edge 1/2 inch above plate. Bake 35 minutes or until crisp and dry. Place on a rack; cool to room temperature. Scoop ice cream into meringue shell; top with chocolate sauce or chocolate syrup. Cut in wedges to serve. Makes 6 to 8 servings.

Cornflake Macaroons

The children were standing in line to sample these as we tested them.

2 egg whites (1/4 cup),
   room temperature
1 cup sugar

1/2 teaspoon vanilla extract
1 cup shredded coconut
2 cups cornflakes

Preheat oven to 275F (135C). Grease 2 large baking sheets. In a medium bowl, beat egg whites with an electric mixer until stiff. Gradually add sugar, 1 tablespoon at a time, beating until mixture is very thick. Fold in vanilla, then fold in coconut and cornflakes. Drop batter by heaping teaspoonfuls onto greased baking sheets, spacing cookies 2 inches apart. Bake 18 to 20 minutes. Cool 5 minutes on baking sheets. Remove from baking sheets; cool completely on racks. Cookies will set as they cool. Makes about 24 cookies.

Chocolate Angel Food Cake

Serve with sweetened whipped cream.

3/4 cup cake flour, sifted 5 times
   before measuring
1/4 cup sifted unsweetened cocoa powder
12 egg whites (1-1/2 cups), room temperature
1/4 teaspoon salt

1 teaspoon cream of tartar
1-1/4 cups sugar
1/2 teaspoon lemon extract
1/2 teaspoon vanilla extract

Preheat oven to 275F (135C). In a small bowl, sift together flour and cocoa powder; set aside. In a large bowl, beat egg whites and salt with an electric mixer until frothy. Add cream of tartar; beat until stiff, but not dry. Fold in sugar, 1 tablespoon at a time, beating constantly. Gradually fold flour mixture into egg-white mixture. Fold in lemon extract and vanilla. Pour batter into an ungreased angel food cake pan. Run a spatula through batter several times to prevent holes. Bake 15 minutes. Increase oven temperature to 300F (150C) and continue to bake about 1 more hour or until top springs back when lightly touched with fingers. Invert hot cake over a bottle; cool completely before removing from pan. Makes 12 to 16 servings.

Whole-Wheat Angel Food Cake

Whole-wheat flour adds extra flavor to this traditional cake.

3/4 cup finely ground whole-wheat flour or
   whole-wheat pastry flour
1/4 cup cornstarch
1-1/2 cups sugar
12 egg whites (1-1/2 cups),
   room temperature
1/2 teaspoon salt

1-1/2 teaspoons cream of tartar
1/2 teaspoon vanilla extract
1/4 teaspoon almond extract
1/2 pint whipping cream (1 cup),
   whipped, sweetened
Fresh fruit in season

Preheat oven to 325F (165C). In a small bowl, sift together flour, cornstarch and 3/4 cup sugar; set aside. In a large bowl, combine egg whites, salt and cream of tartar. Beat with an electric mixer until stiff peaks form. Gradually add remaining 3/4 cup sugar, vanilla and almond extract, beating on low speed; continue to beat until mixture holds stiff peaks. Stop mixer; sift 1/3 of the flour mixture over egg-white mixture. Carefully fold in for just a second; don't fold in thoroughly. Sift 1/2 of remaining flour mixture over egg-white mixture; fold in again for a second. Add remaining flour mixture; fold in just until flour is incorporated. Pour batter into an ungreased angel-food cake pan. Run a spatula through batter several times to prevent holes. Bake 50 to 60 minutes or until a thin skewer inserted in center comes out clean. Invert hot cake over a bottle; cool completely before removing from pan. To serve, slice and top with whipped cream and fresh fruit. Makes 12 to 16 servings.

Variation
White Angel Food Cake: Substitute 3/4 cup all-purpose flour for the 3/4 cup whole-wheat flour.

Individual Meringue Shells

Try forming each meringue in the shape of a heart, then filling with ice cream and strawberries for Valentine's Day.

4 egg whites (1/2 cup),
   room temperature
1/4 teaspoon salt
1 teaspoon vanilla extract
1/2 teaspoon white vinegar

1-1/3 cups sugar
Sliced strawberries
Sweet English Custard Sauce, page 136,
   or vanilla ice cream

Preheat oven to 300F (150C). Line a baking sheet with parchment paper or a brown-paper grocery bag. In a medium bowl, beat egg whites, salt, vanilla and vinegar with an electric mixer until soft peaks form. Gradually add sugar, beating until mixture is very stiff. Drop by very large spoonfuls onto prepared baking sheet. Using back of a large spoon, make a 1/2-inch-deep indentation in middle of each meringue. Bake 45 minutes or until crisp and dry. Cool completely on baking sheet. Fill with strawberries and Sweet English Custard Sauce or ice cream. Makes 8 servings.

Florida Key Lime Soufflé

The perfect light dessert to serve after a rich, filling meal.

1 (1/4-oz.) envelope unflavored
   gelatin (1 tablespoon)
1/4 cup cold water
4 egg yolks (1/3 cup)
2/3 cup fresh lime juice
1/2 cup sugar
1/2 teaspoon salt

1 teaspoon grated lime peel
3 to 6 drops green food coloring,
   if desired
6 egg whites (3/4 cup), room temperature
1/2 cup sugar
1/2 pint whipping cream (1 cup), whipped
Toasted flaked coconut

In a small bowl, soften gelatin in cold water; set aside. Place egg yolks in a small saucepan; beat well with a whisk. Beat in lime juice, 1/2 cup sugar and salt. Cook over low heat, stirring constantly, until slightly thickened. Remove from heat; add softened gelatin, lime peel and food coloring, if desired. Stir until gelatin is completely dissolved; cool. In a large bowl, beat egg whites with an electric mixer until stiff, moist peaks form. Gradually add 1/2 cup sugar, beating until mixture is stiff. Fold in cooled lime mixture and whipped cream. Oil 8 individual dessert or soufflé dishes or a 1-1/2-quart soufflé dish. Pour dessert into oiled dish or dishes. Refrigerate several hours or until set. Garnish with toasted coconut before serving. Makes 8 servings.

Hard-cooked eggs:

Suggestions for use: Use in salad dressings, chef's salads, potato salads, deviled eggs, egg-salad-sandwich filling; add to white sauce and serve over toast or pasta.

Recipes included:

Deviled-Egg Casserole, below

Eggs à la Goldenrod

An excellent dish for an April brunch or light supper — it uses up those leftover hard-cooked Easter eggs.

3 **English muffins, split, toasted, buttered**	3/4 **teaspoon seasoned salt**
9 **hard-cooked eggs, halved**	1/3 **teaspoon pepper**
6 **tablespoons butter or margarine**	1-1/2 **cups shredded Monterey Jack cheese (6 oz.)**
6 **tablespoons all-purpose flour**	7 **bacon slices, crisp-cooked, crumbled**
3 **cups milk**	

Preheat oven to 350F (175C). Place English muffin halves in a single layer in a baking dish. Place 3 egg halves, cut-side down, on top of each muffin half; set aside. In a heavy saucepan, melt butter or margarine over low heat. Stir in flour until blended; cook, stirring constantly, about 1 minute. Slowly add milk, stirring with a whisk until smooth. Continue to cook, stirring constantly, until bubbly and thickened. Then continue to cook and stir 2 more minutes. Stir in seasoned salt and pepper. Pour over eggs and English muffins. Top with cheese and bacon. Bake 15 to 20 minutes or until heated through. Makes 6 servings.

Deviled-Egg Casserole

Leftover hard-cooked eggs and leftover rice are combined in this savory seafood casserole.

4 to 6 **hard-cooked eggs**	1 **(4-1/2-oz.) can small shrimp, rinsed, drained**
1/4 **cup mayonnaise-style salad dressing**	1 **(10-3/4-oz.) can cream of celery soup or cream of onion soup**
2 **teaspoons prepared mustard**	1/2 **cup milk**
1/4 **teaspoon salt**	4 **cups cooked long-grain white rice**
Dash of pepper	
1 **teaspoon sweet pickle relish, if desired**	

Preheat oven to 350F (175C). Butter a 2-quart casserole dish. Cut eggs in half lengthwise; carefully remove yolks. In a small bowl, combine egg yolks, salad dressing, mustard, salt, pepper and pickle relish, if desired. Mash with a fork; stir until smooth. Spoon mixture evenly into egg-white halves; set aside. In a large bowl, combine shrimp, soup and milk; stir to blend. Stir in rice; pour mixture into buttered dish. Gently push deviled eggs, yolk-side up, into rice mixture. Bake 20 to 30 minutes or until heated through. Makes 6 to 8 servings.

Potato skins, cooked potatoes

Suggestions for use: Save potato skins. Toss with melted butter or margarine, salt and favorite seasonings. Bake at 475F (245C) until crisp. Cut leftover baked potatoes in wedges, season and fry in butter; shape leftover mashed potatoes in patties, dip in flour and fry in butter; use leftover mashed potatoes for Norwegian Lefse, add to bread doughs or spudnuts or use to top meat loaves.

Recipes included:
Mashed-Potato Delight, page 96
Norwegian Lefse, below

Norwegian Lefse

Lefse are a great use for leftover mashed potatoes. Your children will love them.

1 cup mashed potatoes
About 2/3 cup all-purpose flour

Butter or margarine, room temperature
Sugar, if desired

Place potatoes in a medium bowl. Add 2/3 cup flour; knead into potatoes to make a stiff dough. Add additional flour if dough is too sticky to handle. Divide dough into 5 portions; shape each into a ball. Preheat an electric griddle to 375F (190C) or heat a large skillet over medium heat. On a lightly floured surface or pastry cloth, roll 1 ball of dough to a paper-thin 8-inch circle. Repeat with remaining 4 balls. Place dough circles on ungreased hot griddle or skillet; cook 1 to 2 minutes per side or until browned in spots. Cooked lefse should still be flexible. Spread warm lefse with butter or margarine; sprinkle with sugar, if desired. To serve, roll up and cut diagonally into 2-inch slices; or fold in quarters. If preparing ahead, wrap cooked lefse individually in plastic wrap to prevent drying; refrigerate up to 3 days. Or freeze wrapped lefse up to 6 weeks. To reheat, unwrap lefse. Bake in a 300F (150C) oven, 10 to 15 minutes. Makes 4 or 5 servings.

How to Make Norwegian Lefse

1/On a lightly floured surface, roll 1 ball of dough to a paper-thin 8-inch circle. Repeat with remaining balls of dough.

2/Bake on a griddle or in a skillet 1 to 2 minutes per side or until browned in spots. Cooked lefse will still be flexible. Butter, sprinkle with sugar or spread with jam then roll up to eat.

Rice

Suggestions for use: Use in puddings, salads, soups, meatballs, meat loaves, casseroles; use as a filling for cabbage rolls.

Recipes included:

Deviled-Egg Casserole, page 140

Rice Pudding with Raspberry Sauce

This old "pioneer" recipe has been a favorite of ours for years.

2 cups cooked long-grain white rice
1/4 teaspoon salt
1-3/4 cups milk or half and half
2/3 cup sugar

1/2 teaspoon almond extract
Raspberry Sauce, see below
1/2 pint whipping cream (1 cup), whipped

Raspberry Sauce:

1 (10-oz.) pkg. frozen raspberries, thawed, undrained
1/3 cup water
2 tablespoons cornstarch

2 tablespoons cold water
1/4 cup sugar
1 tablespoon lemon juice

In a medium saucepan, combine rice, salt and milk or half and half. Cover; simmer, stirring occasionally, 25 to 30 minutes or until mixture is thickened. Remove from heat; stir in sugar and almond extract. Cover; refrigerate until well chilled. Prepare Raspberry Sauce; set aside. Just before serving, fold whipped cream into rice mixture. Serve in bowls; top with Raspberry Sauce. Makes 6 servings.

Raspberry Sauce:

In a small saucepan, combine raspberries and 1/3 cup water. In a small bowl, mix cornstarch with 2 tablespoons cold water. Add to raspberry mixture. Add sugar. Cook over medium heat, stirring, until thickened and bubbly. Remove from heat; stir in lemon juice. Cover until ready to serve.

Metric Chart

Comparison to Metric Measure

When You Know	Symbol	Multiply By	To Find	Symbol
teaspoons	tsp	5.0	milliliters	ml
tablespoons	tbsp	15.0	milliliters	ml
fluid ounces	fl. oz.	30.0	milliliters	ml
cups	c	0.24	liters	l
pints	pt.	0.47	liters	l
quarts	qt.	0.95	liters	l
ounces	oz.	28.0	grams	g
pounds	lb.	0.45	kilograms	kg
Fahrenheit	F	5/9 (after subtracting 32)	Celsius	C

Liquid Measure to Liters

1/4 cup	=	0.06 liters
1/2 cup	=	0.12 liters
3/4 cup	=	0.18 liters
1 cup	=	0.24 liters
1-1/4 cups	=	0.3 liters
1-1/2 cups	=	0.36 liters
2 cups	=	0.48 liters
2-1/2 cups	=	0.6 liters
3 cups	=	0.72 liters
3-1/2 cups	=	0.84 liters
4 cups	=	0.96 liters
4-1/2 cups	=	1.08 liters
5 cups	=	1.2 liters
5-1/2 cups	=	1.32 liters

Liquid Measure to Milliliters

1/4 teaspoon	=	1.25 milliliters
1/2 teaspoon	=	2.5 milliliters
3/4 teaspoon	=	3.75 milliliters
1 teaspoon	=	5.0 milliliters
1-1/4 teaspoons	=	6.25 milliliters
1-1/2 teaspoons	=	7.5 milliliters
1-3/4 teaspoons	=	8.75 milliliters
2 teaspoons	=	10.0 milliliters
1 tablespoon	=	15.0 milliliters
2 tablespoons	=	30.0 milliliters

Fahrenheit to Celsius

F	C
200—205	95
220—225	105
245—250	120
275	135
300—305	150
325—330	165
345—350	175
370—375	190
400—405	205
425—430	220
445—450	230
470—475	245
500	260

Index